BORING BIBLE

INSTANT LESSON
MATERIAL

ABRAHAM TO JACOB

ANDY ROBB

kevin
mayhew

First published in 2003 by
KEVIN MAYHEW LTD
Buxhall, Stowmarket, Suffolk, IP14 3BW
www.kevinmayhew.com

9 8 7 6 5 4 3 2

ISBN-13: 978 1 84417 072 2
ISBN-10: 1 84417 072 1
Catalogue No 1500588

Cover illustration by Andy Robb
Cover design by Angela Selfe
Typesetting by Andy Robb
Printed and bound in Great Britain

CONTENTS

HOW TO USE THIS BOOK

As far as most kids are concerned, the Bible is probably the most mind-numbingly boring book they could think of.

But what's even *more* surprising is that most of them have never even read the teensiest snatch of the book.

In fact, most kids wouldn't know their Gideon from their Goliath if it hit them right between the eyes! (Sorry about the analogy.)

So, when it comes to teaching them a thing or two about some of the stuff that's *in* the Bible then you're probably better off giving them the option of revising for a maths test or going to the opera.

Let's face it – for most kids the Bible is just one big turn-off, which is a shame because it's the one book that's going to help them make some sort of sense of their young lives.

So if you happen to be landed with (I mean have the privilege of) unpacking the Bible to kids then the task set before you can seem like an uphill struggle.

Fear not!

That's where the **Boring Bible Instant Lesson Material** comes in.

These books provide you with a fresh and a fun way to bring to life familiar (or perhaps hard to understand) Bible stories in a handy, ready-to-use format and in a way that will appeal to kids.

Each book contains **25 Bible stories** to choose from and features a snapshot of the background to each Bible passage selected, the key characters involved and Bible passage reproduced in its entirety.

All this appears on the left-hand side of each double page spread which is purely for your consumption.

On the facing page is the material that's designed totally with the kids in mind and retells the Bible passage in the inimitable Boring Bible style. (High on humour – low on waffle.)

So, now that you've parted with money for this book, how exactly do you use it?

SOME SERVING SUGGESTIONS

Because the situations and circumstances of every purchaser of this book vary, there are no hard and fast rules as to how to make the most of the **Boring Bible Instant Lesson Material**.

You may, for instance, be covering one or more of the featured Bible stories in a school setting.

Alternatively, you may be a Sunday school teacher.

The material in this book might aid you to deliver a complete Bible teaching session or perhaps simply to enhance or supplement something you've already prepared.

Either way, this book should make your task easier – and more fun!

Here are some suggestions:

- Give the kids a quick overview of the Bible passage you've selected (as explained in the teacher's page), read them the Bible passage and then hand out photocopies of the kids' pages for them to read on their own.

  If you've got time to spare, how about allowing them to colour in the cartoon picture?

- Explain the background to the Bible story, hand out photocopies of the kids' page and then you read it out while they follow it.

  You could even put the cartoon picture on an OHP to display at the relevant point in the story.

- Perhaps you're doing an upfront kids' talk at church and need to retell a Bible passage in a way that engages the kids.

  Why not use the kids' page as your script and pop the cartoon picture on to an OHP?

- Or if you've been teaching on one of the featured Bible passages in this book then why not use the kids' page as a take-home sheet to act as a handy reminder of what they've learned.

No doubt you'll find other creative ways to use this book but the bottom line is that it's here to make your job easier and for the kids to have a clearer understanding of what the Bible is about and what it has to say to them.

Have fun!

GOD CALLS ABRAM

WHAT'S IT ALL ABOUT?

This Bible story is about Abram and how God called him to pack his bags and head for a new home in Canaan

WHO ARE THE MAIN CHARACTERS?

Abram. His wife Sarai, his nephew Lot and his slaves also get a mention

WHERE'S IT FOUND IN THE BIBLE?

Genesis 12:1-9

HERE'S THE BIBLE PASSAGE...

The Lord said to Abram, 'Leave your country, your relatives, and your father's home, and go to a land that I am going to show you. I will give you many descendants, and they will become a great nation. I will bless you and make your name famous, so that you will be a blessing. I will bless those who bless you, but I will curse those who curse you.

'And through you I will bless all the nations.'

When Abram was 75 years old, he started out from Haran, as the Lord had told him to do; and Lot went with him. Abram took his wife Sarai, his nephew Lot, and all the wealth and all the slaves they had acquired in Haran, and they started out for the land of Canaan. When they arrived in Canaan, Abram travelled through the land until he came to the sacred tree of Moreh, the holy place at Shechem. (At that time the Canaanites were still living in the land.) The Lord appeared to Abram and said to him, 'This is the country that I am going to give to your descendants.' Then Abram built an altar there to the Lord, who had appeared to him. After that, he moved on south to the hill country east of the city of Bethel and set up his camp between Bethel on the west and Ai on the east. There also he built an altar and worshipped the Lord. Then he moved on from place to place, going towards the southern part of Canaan.

STAR TREK!

Wanna be rich and famous? Well the **star** of *this* story (Abram) hadn't really given it a second thought. (Probably 'cos he wasn't short of a bob or two to start with, but that's **not the point**.) The point *is* that Abram wasn't looking for a fast buck or for that matter desperate to have his photo splashed all over the front page of every celebrity magazine. Okay, so celebrity magazines and photos hadn't quite been invented yet but if they *had* what's the guessing that old Abram wouldn't have been in the *least* bit interested. Did I say *old* Abram? Oh yes, I forgot to tell you. Abram's *already* **75 years old** before he even gets his big break in the Bible. The way it happened was like this.

Abram was living in a place called **Haran** when he got an unexpected call from none other than **God**.

The gist of the conversation was that God told Abram to pack up, leave town and head for **Canaan** (about 500 miles away, if you must know).

The *good* thing was that Abram did what God said – which is probably why God picked him in the first place! Along with his wife (Sarai), his nephew Lot and all his wealth and slaves he **trekked** down to the wonderful land of Canaan.

I don't know about *you* but when I get to the end of a long journey all *I* feel like doing is putting my feet up or having a swim in the pool (if it's my hols). Not Abram! He just kept on going until he reached a particularly special tree. Why was it special? Easy! 'Cos God was planning to meet up with him there. And guess what? God had *another* message for Abram. *This* time he told Abram that he was going to give Canaan to Abram and his descendants to **live in**. What? The *whole* land?!

Personally I'd have settled for a patch just big enough to grow a few carrots and potatoes but Abram was handed every **last inch** of Canaan – on a plate. **Jammy or what?**

The Bible says that Abram built an altar (a pile of stones which you burn animal sacrifices on) there and worshipped God. From then on in, Abram moved from place to place around the land of Canaan. (There are *some* advantages to living in tents – but not many!)

One last thing. You're probably wondering why on earth God made Abram leave Haran in the *first* place aren't you? Well, to put it in a nutshell, God had a **whopper of a plan** up his sleeve which involved starting up a **brand-new nation**.

And guess *who* had the job of getting it up and running? Yep, **Abram**.

ABRAM AND LOT SEPARATE

WHAT'S IT ALL ABOUT?

This Bible story is about how Abram and Lot had to part company to avoid getting under each other's feet

WHO ARE THE MAIN CHARACTERS?

Abram and Lot are centre stage with their servants playing bit parts. And not forgetting their flocks

WHERE'S IT FOUND IN THE BIBLE?

Genesis 13:1-13

HERE'S THE BIBLE PASSAGE...

Abram went north out of Egypt to the southern part of Canaan with his wife and everything he owned, and Lot went with him. Abram was a very rich man, with sheep, goats, and cattle, as well as silver and gold. Then he left there and moved from place to place, going towards Bethel. He reached the place between Bethel and Ai where he had camped before and had built an altar. There he worshipped the Lord.

Lot also had sheep, goats, and cattle, as well as his own family and servants. And so there was not enough pasture land for the two of them to stay together, because they had too many animals.

So quarrels broke out between the men who took care of Abram's animals and those who took care of Lot's animals. (At that time the Canaanites and the Perizzites were still living in the land.)

Then Abram said to Lot, 'We are relatives, and your men and my men shouldn't be quarrelling. So let's separate. Choose any part of the land you want. You go one way, and I'll go the other.'

Lot looked around and saw that the whole Jordan Valley, all the way to Zoar, had plenty of water, like the Garden of the Lord or like the land of Egypt. (This was before the Lord had destroyed the cities of Sodom and Gomorrah.) So Lot chose the whole Jordan Valley for himself and moved away towards the east. That is how the two men parted. Abram stayed in the land of Canaan, and Lot settled among the cities in the valley and camped near Sodom, whose people were wicked and sinned against the Lord.

CHOCK-A-BLOCK!

When it comes to **big names** in the Bible, **Abram**'s out there in front with the best of them. We catch up with him after a short break in **Egypt** where he's been avoiding a rather nasty famine that decided to drop by and say 'hello' to the land of Canaan (where he was living). Abram eventually got the all-clear to return (which he did) together with his wife, his nephew Lot and everything he owned (which was heaps, I can tell you – sheep, goats, cattle, silver, gold, you name it, *he* had it. OK, so he didn't have a *Playstation* but you know what I mean!). Being the travelling man that he was (he lived in a tent), Abram and co. drifted from place to place until they ended up right where they'd started a few years back, somewhere between **Bethel** and **Ai**. Being the sort of chap who respected God, Abram had built an altar on the spot when he'd camped there before, and, not one to miss a recycling opportunity, Abram put it to good use once again. The Bible tells us that Abram worshipped God there.

Then the **trouble** began. Not *only* did Abram have loads of sheep, goats and cattle but so did his nephew Lot. The hillsides were **chock-a-block** full of them and it wasn't long before Abram and Lot's servants started to **quarrel**.

Abram and Lot were having *none* of it. The last thing *they* needed was a **big family row**.

Uncle Abram had an idea. Seeing that there wasn't enough pasture for all their animals to graze on the best thing was to go their separate ways.

OK, so there were still plenty of **Canaanites** living in the land but that still left *loads* of places that both Abram and Lot could live *without* treading on each other's toes.

After a quick look around Lot decided to head for the **Jordan Valley**.

As far as he could make out it looked just **perfect**.

Loads of water, lush countryside, lots of food.

Just the job – or so Lot *thought*!

In *another* Bible story about Lot you can find out that appearances can *sometimes* be very **deceptive**.

But perhaps more of that later. As for good old Abram, well, Abram sort of stayed put, right where he was. Abram was a man who liked to do what **God** says and because God had said that he'd got to live in Canaan, that's *exactly* what he did.

That's it for now, but that's not the *last* you've heard of Abram – in fact, it's just **the beginning**.

ABRAM RESCUES LOT

WHAT'S IT ALL ABOUT?

This Bible story is about how Abram rescued his nephew Lot from five invading kings

WHO ARE THE MAIN CHARACTERS?

Abram is the hero but there's Lot (of course) plus nine kings (five on one side and four on the other)

WHERE'S IT FOUND IN THE BIBLE?

Genesis 14:1-16

HERE'S THE BIBLE PASSAGE...

Four kings, Amraphel of Babylonia, Arioch of Ellasar, Chedorlaomer of Elam, and Tidal of Goiim, went to war against five other kings: Bera of Sodom, Birsha of Gomorrah, Shinab of Admah, Shemeber of Zeboiim, and the king of Bela (or Zoar). These five kings had formed an alliance and joined forces in the Valley of Siddim, which is now the Dead Sea. They had been under the control of Chedorlaomer for twelve years, but in the thirteenth year they rebelled against him. In the fourteenth year Chedorlaomer and his allies came with their armies and defeated the Rephaim in Ashteroth Karnaim, the Zuzim in Ham, the Emim in the plain of Kiriathaim, and the Horites in the mountains of Edom, pursuing them as far as Elparan on the edge of the desert. Then they turned round and came back to Kadesh (then known as Enmishpat). They conquered all the land of the Amalekites and defeated the Amorites who lived in Hazazon Tamar.

Then the kings of Sodom, Gomorrah, Admah, Zeboiim, and Bela drew up their armies for battle in the Valley of Siddim and fought against the kings of Elam, Goiim, Babylonia, and Ellasar, five kings against four. The valley was full of tar pits, and when the kings of Sodom and Gomorrah tried to run away from the battle, they fell into the pits; but the other three kings escaped to the mountains. The four kings took everything in Sodom and Gomorrah, including the food, and went away. Lot, Abram's nephew, was living in Sodom, so they took him and all his possessions.

But a man escaped and reported all this to Abram, the Hebrew, who was living near the sacred trees belonging to Mamre the Amorite. Mamre and his brothers Eshcol and Aner were Abram's allies. When Abram heard that his nephew had been captured, he called together all the fighting men in his camp, 318 in all, and pursued the four kings all the way to Dan. There he divided his men into groups, attacked the enemy by night, and defeated them. He chased them as far as Hobah, north of Damascus, and recovered the loot that had been taken. He also brought back his nephew Lot and his possessions, together with the women and the other prisoners.

TAR VERY MUCH!

Abram's nephew **Lot** had probably thought he'd fallen on his feet when he settled in the luscious (green and fertile) city of Sodom. He was about to find out that he couldn't have been *more* **wrong**. Four kings from up north were heading in *his* direction and this wasn't going to be a *friendly* royal visit. The kings who ruled Sodom (and thereabouts) had told a guy called **Chedorlaomer** to get off their backs. He'd been ruling over *them* for 12 years and they'd had enough. Chedorlaomer (and three other kings) wasted no time in setting out to pay a visit to these 'rebellious' kings.

Not confused yet, are you? Good! Just keep concentrating 'cos things are about to **hot up**.

The **four kings** surged south and woe-betide *anyone* who got in their way (such as the people of Ashteroth Karnaim, Ham, Kiriathaim, Edom and Hazazon Tamar who got *well*-pummelled).

At long last it was time for the **four kings** to lay into the rebellious **five kings**. (Five against four doesn't sound fair does it? But that's war for you!) One thing the *five* kings seemed to have forgotten about their chosen battleground (the **Valley of Siddim**) was that it had more than its fair share of **tar pits**.

When the kings of Sodom and Gomorrah tried to run away (the other three had already hot-footed it to the mountains) they fell into the tar pits and **got stuck**!

IT MIGHT SOUND FUNNY TO YOU BUT MY WIFE'LL KILL ME IF I COME HOME LOOKING LIKE THIS!

With the kings of Sodom and Gomorrah coming to a **sticky end** (literally!) the four kings just walked right in and captured *everything* they could lay their hands on. Which included **Lot** and all his possessions.

Abram soon got wind of what had happened to his nephew (thanks to a man who'd managed to escape). Abram wasted no time in getting together an army of his own (OK, so it was just **318 fighting men** but let's still call it an army, shall we? It sounds better).

Abram wasn't alone. **Mamre the Amorite** along with his brothers Eschol and Aner had the odd score or two that they wanted to settle with Chedorlaomer and his cronies, so *they* came along too. Abram and his 'army' pursued the four kings all the way to **Dan**.

Using a bit of cunning military strategy, Abram split his men into **groups** and attacked the unsuspecting enemy at night and **defeated them**.

Hurray! Just to make *sure* they'd got the message Abram and his fighting men chased them all the way to **Hobah** (which was way up north).

Not *only* did Abram rescue Lot but he also successfully recovered Lot's family, servants and possessions. Not a bad day's work, though I say it myself! And I'll bet *you* didn't think someone as old as Abram had it *in* him, did you?

ABRAM'S VISION

WHAT'S IT ALL ABOUT?

This Bible story is about how God promises Abram that one day he'll have a son of his own to inherit his wealth

WHO ARE THE MAIN CHARACTERS?

Abram and God headline with Eliezer getting a mention.
Oh yes . . . a cow, a goat, a ram, a pigeon and a dove as well

WHERE'S IT FOUND IN THE BIBLE?

Genesis 15:1-21

HERE'S THE BIBLE PASSAGE...

After this, Abram had a vision and heard the Lord say to him, 'Do not be afraid, Abram. I will shield you from danger and give you a great reward.' But Abram answered, 'Sovereign Lord, what good will your reward do me, since I have no children? My only heir is Eliezer of Damascus. You have given me no children, and one of my slaves will inherit my property.'

Then he heard the Lord speaking to him again: 'This slave Eliezer will not inherit your property; your own son will be your heir.' The Lord took him outside and said, 'Look at the sky and try to count the stars; you will have as many descendants as that.'

Abram put his trust in the Lord, and because of this the Lord was pleased with him and accepted him. Then the Lord said to him, 'I am the Lord, who led you out of Ur in Babylonia, to give you this land as your own.'

But Abram asked, 'Sovereign Lord, how can I know that it will be mine?'

He answered, 'Bring me a cow, a goat, and a ram, each of them three years old, and a dove and a pigeon.' Abram brought the animals to God, cut them in half, and placed the halves opposite each other in two rows; but he did not cut up the birds.

Vultures came down on the bodies, but Abram drove them off. When the sun was going down, Abram fell into a deep sleep, and fear and terror came over him. The Lord said to him, 'Your descendants will be strangers in a foreign land; they will be slaves there and will be treated cruelly for four hundred years. But I will punish the nation that enslaves them, and when they leave that foreign land, they will take great wealth with them. You yourself will live to a ripe old age, die in peace, and be buried. It will be four generations before your descendants come back here, because I will not drive out the Amorites until they become so wicked that they must be punished.'

When the sun had set and it was dark, a smoking fire-pot and a flaming torch suddenly appeared and passed between the pieces of the animals. Then and there the Lord made a covenant with Abram. He said, 'I promise to give your descendants all this land from the border of Egypt to the River Euphrates, including the lands of the Kenites, the Kenizzites, the Kadmonites, the Hittites, the Perizzites, the Rephaim, the Amorites, the Canaanites, the Girgashites, and the Jebusites.'

PROMISES, PROMISES!

Abram was no ordinary fella. God had **big plans** for him but *sometimes* he needed a bit of a gentle reminder that what God had *said* was going to happen really *would*. Which is probably why God suddenly appeared to Abram in a **vision**.

Not only *that* but God had a few things he wanted to *say* to our hero.

'I will shield you from danger and give you a great reward,' God told Abram. **A great reward**? Sounds good to me! But Abram couldn't see the *point* in God giving him *any* sort of **freebee** if he didn't have any kids to pass it on to when he died.

And to be honest, Abram wasn't too keen on the idea of his slave, **Eliezer,** inheriting all his worldly wealth. Never fear, Abram. God's thought of *that* already.

God (or the **Lord**, as the Bible puts it) took Abram outside and told him to look up at the sky and have a shot at **counting the star**s.

ONE MILLION TWO HUNDRED AND THIRTY TWO THOUSAND FIVE HUNDRED AND TWENTY FOUR, ONE MILLION TWO HUNDRED AND THIRTY TWO THOUSAND FIVE HUNDRED AND ... OH NO! I'VE GONE AND LOST COUNT! I'LL HAVE TO START ALL OVER AGAIN! ONE, TWO THREE ...

Whether Abram actually got *round* to counting **every last star** is *anyone's* guess but the long and the short of it was that Abram put his **trust in God** which was a **good move** because the Bible tells us that God was **pleased** with him for doing that.

(At least now we know how to *please* God, don't we?)

One thing was puzzling Abram. How could he be absolutely *certain* that all this would happen and that his descendants *would* take possession of the land of Canaan (like God had *also* promised)?

Before God gave Abram his answer he instructed him to cut in half a cow, a goat and a ram. (Dead ones, obviously!) As the sun began to set, Abram fell into a **deep sleep** and once again God spoke to him.

God told Abram that his **descendants** would be held as **slaves** in a **foreign land** for **four hundred years** but when they were set free they'd take **great wealth** with them.

God *also* told Abram that he would live to a ripe old age and die in peace.

As night fell, the Bible says that a **smoking pot** and a **flaming torch** appeared and passed between the cut up pieces of animal.

It was *God's* way of making a covenant (an unbreakable promise) with Abram that *everything* he'd promised really *would* happen.

Awesome or what?!

HAGAR AND ISHMAEL

WHAT'S IT ALL ABOUT?

This Bible story is about how Abram tried to pre-empt God and produce his promised son, but by his slave girl, not his wife

WHO ARE THE MAIN CHARACTERS?

Abram, Sarai, Hagar (the slave-girl) and Ishmael all feature – along with a helpful angel

WHERE'S IT FOUND IN THE BIBLE?

Genesis 16:1-16

HERE'S THE BIBLE PASSAGE...

Abram's wife Sarai had not borne him any children. But she had an Egyptian slave woman named Hagar, and so she said to Abram, 'The Lord has kept me from having children. Why don't you sleep with my slave? Perhaps she can have a child for me.' Abram agreed with what Sarai said. So she gave Hagar to him to be his concubine. (This happened after Abram had lived in Canaan for 10 years.) Abram had intercourse with Hagar, and she became pregnant. When she found out that she was pregnant, she became proud and despised Sarai. Then Sarai said to Abram, 'It's your fault that Hagar despises me. I myself gave her to you, and ever since she found out that she was pregnant, she has despised me. May the Lord judge which of us is right, you or me!'

Abram answered, 'Very well, she is your slave and under your control; do whatever you want with her.' Then Sarai treated Hagar so cruelly that she ran away.

The angel of the Lord met Hagar at a spring in the desert on the road to Shur and said, 'Hagar, slave of Sarai, where have you come from and where are you going?' She answered, 'I am running away from my mistress.'

He said, 'Go back to her and be her slave.' Then he said, 'I will give you so many descendants that no one will be able to count them. You are going to have a son, and you will name him Ishmael, because the Lord has heard your cry of distress. But your son will live like a wild donkey; he will be against everyone, and everyone will be against him. He will live apart from all his relatives.'

Hagar asked herself, 'Have I really seen God and lived to tell about it?' So she called the Lord who had spoken to her 'A God who Sees'. That is why people call the well between Kadesh and Bered 'The Well of the Living One who Sees Me'.

Hagar bore Abram a son, and he named him Ishmael. Abram was 86 years old at the time.

WILD CHILD!

Abram and his wife (**Sarai**) were (not to be *too* rude) getting on a bit and they *still* didn't have any kids. The problem was that **God** had promised **Abram** that his descendants would be as **numerous as the stars in the sky**. And for *that* a son and heir would be really handy – in fact, very *necessary*. So Abram decided to take matters into his *own* hands.

To be fair to Abram, Sarai was giving him a bit of a hard time moaning about the lack of kids. 'Why not have a child by our slave girl, **Hagar**,' she suggested. (They did that sort of thing in those days.)

So being the obedient sort of hubbie that he was, Abram duly obliged and Hagar fell pregnant.

Things didn't go *quite* the way Sarai had planned and Hagar started to get ideas above her station. To put it bluntly, she started to despise her mistress (Sarai) which really cheesed Sarai off **something rotten**.

Poor old Abram took the brunt of it.

Sarai was **well miffed** and she let her husband know about it in *no* uncertain terms.

IT'S ALL YOUR FAULT ... NAG, NAG, NAG, NAG ... I GAVE HER TO YOU AND NOW SHE DESPISES ME ... NAG, NAG, NAG, NAG ... MAY THE LORD JUDGE WHICH IS RIGHT, YOU OR ME ... NAG, NAG, NAG ...!

Abram did what *every* right-minded husband would do for a quiet life. 'Do whatever you want with her', he told Sarai.

That's a bit of a cop-out if you ask me. But *Sarai* didn't mess around. She treated Hagar so **cruelly** that the poor slave girl **ran away**.

Fortunately for her, God had seen everything that had been going on and figured that Hagar had had a bit of a **raw deal** to say the least. God dispatched an **angel** to rendezvous with the slave girl while she rested at a **desert spring**.

The angel told Hagar to go back and be Sarai's slave. A bit like God promised Abram, the angel promised Hagar that she would have so *many* descendants you wouldn't be able to *count* them.

A *son* did you say? Hey, that means Hagar knew the sex of her child before it was born.

And added to which she didn't even have to think up a name for him – *God* had thought of *that* as well.

He was going to be called **Ishmael** but the bad news was that he was going to be like a wild donkey and was going to be against e*veryone* – *including* Abram's descendants.

The Bible says that Abram was **86 years old** when Ishmael was born (a *young* 86, obviously!) but by the sound of it he was probably going to regret taking things into his *own* hands and *not* waiting for **God** to give him **a son** by his wife, Sarai.

THE COVENANT OF CIRCUMCISION

WHAT'S IT ALL ABOUT?

This Bible story is about how God introduced the custom of circumcision to Abram and his male descendants

WHO ARE THE MAIN CHARACTERS?

God and Abram.
Also lucky Ishmael who gets to try out this new custom

WHERE'S IT FOUND IN THE BIBLE?

Genesis 17:1-27

HERE'S THE BIBLE PASSAGE...

When Abram was 99 years old, the Lord appeared to him and said, 'I am the Almighty God. Obey me and always do what is right. I will make my covenant with you and give you many descendants.' Abram bowed down with his face touching the ground, and God said, 'I make this covenant with you: I promise that you will be the ancestor of many nations. Your name will no longer be Abram, but Abraham, because I am making you the ancestor of many nations. I will give you many descendants, and some of them will be kings. You will have so many descendants that they will become nations.

'I will keep my promise to you and to your descendants in future generations as an everlasting covenant. I will be your God and the God of your descendants. I will give to you and to your descendants this land in which you are now a foreigner. The whole land of Canaan will belong to your descendants for ever, and I will be their God.'

God said to Abraham, 'You also must agree to keep the covenant with me, both you and your descendants in future generations. You and your descendants must all agree to circumcise every male among you. From now on you must circumcise every baby boy when he is eight days old, including slaves born in your homes and slaves bought from foreigners. This will show that there is a covenant between you and me. Each one must be circumcised, and this will be a physical sign to show that my covenant with you is everlasting. Any male who

has not been circumcised will no longer be considered one of my people, because he has not kept the covenant with me.' God said to Abraham, 'You must no longer call your wife Sarai; from now on her name is Sarah. I will bless her, and I will give you a son by her. I will bless her, and she will become the mother of nations, and there will be kings among her descendants.' Abraham bowed down with his face touching the ground, but he began to laugh when he thought, 'Can a man have a child when he is a hundred years old? Can Sarah have a child at ninety?' He asked God, 'Why not let Ishmael be my heir?'

But God said, 'No. Your wife Sarah will bear you a son and you will name him Isaac. I will keep my covenant with him and with his descendants for ever. It is an everlasting covenant. I have heard your request about Ishmael, so I will bless him and give him many children and many descendants. He will be the father of twelve princes, and I will make a great nation of his descendants. But I will keep my covenant with your son Isaac, who will be born to Sarah about this time next year.' When God finished speaking to Abraham, he left him.

On that same day Abraham obeyed God and circumcised his son Ishmael and all the other males in his household, including the slaves born in his home and those he had bought. Abraham was 99 years old when he was circumcised, and his son Ishmael was thirteen. They were both circumcised on the same day, together with all Abraham's slaves.

OOCH!

If you know *anything* about **Abram** then you'll know that he had more than his fair share of visits from **God**. *This* story is no exception. Just one year to go before he was a **hundred** and the **Lord God** turned up right in front of Abram. There was nothing for it but for Abram to bow down face first on the ground. When you meet with God there's no messing around!

God wasted no time in reminding Abram of a whole lot of stuff that he knew already, like he'd be the **ancestor of many nations**, that he'd have **many descendants** and that his descendants would live in the **land of Canaan** just like he'd promised Abram already.

Now it was *Abram's* turn to make some promises. OK, so *God* was **100 per cent committed** to *Abram* – now it was Abram's turn to nail *his* colours to the mast and commit *himself* to God.

How was he gonna do that? Easy! God told Abram that every baby boy was to be **circumcised** when they were eight days old. This was going to be a sort of **sign** that Abram's descendants **belonged to God**.

I'll bet you're wondering what **circumcision** is, aren't you? Well, how shall I put it? It's a sort mini operation where a bit of skin is cut off a certain part of your body . . . a certain part of your body that only **boys** have.

Got the picture?

Moving on quickly before you have too much time to think about circumcision, let me tell you about something *else* God told Abram.

Abram was going to have a **name change**. From now on he would be known as **Abraham** (which sounds like the Hebrew word for '**ancestor of many nations**', which is jolly convenient because that's *precisely* what God had lined up for him).

But it wasn't only *Abram* (or should I say Abraham) who was having a change of name – *Sarai* was as well.

God told Abraham that from now on *she* was to be called **Sarah**.

And there was one last (but very *important*) thing that God had to tell Abraham. The bottom line was that God was going to give Sarah a son by Abraham and he was to be called **Isaac**.

Now, *here's* a question. What would *your* reaction be if you were **99** and your wife was **90** and God told you that you were going to have a child?

Well let me tell you what *Abraham* did. **He burst out laughing.** OK, so he was bowed down with his face touching the ground, but he just couldn't help having a little **chuckle** at the very *thought* of it.

Abraham even dared to suggest to God that perhaps *Ishmael* should be his heir but God was having *none* of it.

Abraham humbly went along with what God was saying and followed it through by having all the males in his household circumcised that *very* day.

THE THREE VISITORS

WHAT'S IT ALL ABOUT?

This Bible story is about when three angels turned up at Abraham's place and predicted he'd have a son before very long

WHO ARE THE MAIN CHARACTERS?

The three angels, Abraham, Sarah and a tender calf

WHERE'S IT FOUND IN THE BIBLE?

Genesis 18:1-15

HERE'S THE BIBLE PASSAGE...

The Lord appeared to Abraham at the sacred trees of Mamre. As Abraham was sitting at the entrance of his tent during the hottest part of the day, he looked up and saw three men standing there. As soon as he saw them, he ran out to meet them. Bowing down with his face touching the ground, he said, 'Sirs, please do not pass by my home without stopping; I am here to serve you. Let me bring some water for you to wash your feet; you can rest here beneath this tree. I will also bring a bit of food; it will give you strength to continue your journey. You have honoured me by coming to my home, so let me serve you.' They replied, 'Thank you; we accept.'

Abraham hurried into the tent and said to Sarah, 'Quick, take a sack of your best flour, and bake some bread.' Then he ran to the herd and picked out a calf that was tender and fat, and gave it to a servant, who hurried to get it ready. He took some cream, some milk, and the meat, and set the food before the men. There under the tree he served them himself, and they ate. Then they asked him, 'Where is your wife Sarah?'

'She is there in the tent,' he answered.

One of them said, 'Nine months from now I will come back, and your wife Sarah will have a son.'

Sarah was behind him, at the door of the tent, listening. Abraham and Sarah were very old, and Sarah had stopped having her monthly periods. So Sarah laughed to herself and said, 'Now that I am old and worn out, can I still enjoy sex? And besides, my husband is old too.'

Then the Lord asked Abraham, 'Why did Sarah laugh and say, "Can I really have a child when I am so old?" Is anything too hard for the Lord? As I said, nine months from now I will return, and Sarah will have a son.'

Because Sarah was afraid, she denied it. 'I didn't laugh,' she said.

'Yes, you did,' he replied. 'You laughed.'

THE LAST LAUGH!

Abraham and his wife **Sarah** had been promised a **son** by God, even though they were *well* past it when it came to having kids (let alone bringing them up!). Abraham was pushing **one hundred** and Sarah was only **ten years** behind.

One mega hot day (so the Bible tells us), Abraham was sitting at the entrance to his tent when **three guys** suddenly appeared. Braving the midday sun, Abraham sped over to them (as fast as a **99 year old** *can*!) and fell flat on his face in front of them. No, he *hadn't* tripped over his sandal straps!

There was something **special** about these men that compelled Abraham to **bow down** before them.

Abraham begged the men to come and have a **meal** and to rest themselves for a bit. Taking up Abraham's offer of hospitality they sat down in the shade of a large tree while Abraham quickly rushed off to get Sarah up and running with the cooking arrangements.

Fortunately for the three visitors, Abraham had already planned the menu. Fresh-baked bread, tender calf, milk and cream. **Yum!**

The guests tucked in and when they'd finished one of the men asked Abraham 'Where is your wife Sarah?'

'She's there in the tent' replied Abraham.

Hang on a minute! How did the man know the name of Abraham's wife? I'm beginning to suspect that these guys are more than your run-of-the-mill nomads. There's something *unusual* about them. Back at the tent and with her cooking chores done, Sarah was pinning back her lugholes trying to catch what was being said.

When one of the visitors then announced to Abraham that **nine months** from that *very* day Sarah would give **birth to a son** it was all Sarah could do to stop herself **exploding with laughter**.

Just the *thought* of a worn-out old lady like her having a kid, let alone her ancient husband having anything to do with the matter was enough to start a **fit of the giggles**.

'Why did Sarah laugh?' asked one of the men. 'Is anything too hard for the Lord?'

Suddenly Sarah became frightened. She realised that these weren't just ordinary men – they were **angels sent from God**. 'I didn't laugh', said Sarah.

But everyone knew she *had*.

ABRAHAM PLEADS FOR SODOM

WHAT'S IT ALL ABOUT?

This Bible story is about how Abraham pleads with God not to destroy Sodom if not everyone who lives there is rotten to the core

WHO ARE THE MAIN CHARACTERS?

Abraham and three angels

WHERE'S IT FOUND IN THE BIBLE?

Genesis 18:16-33

HERE'S THE BIBLE PASSAGE...

Then the men left and went to a place where they could look down at Sodom, and Abraham went with them to send them on their way. And the Lord said to himself, 'I will not hide from Abraham what I am going to do. His descendants will become a great and mighty nation, and through him I will bless all the nations. I have chosen him in order that he may command his sons and his descendants to obey me and to do what is right and just. If they do, I will do everything for him that I have promised.'

Then the Lord said to Abraham, 'There are terrible accusations against Sodom and Gomorrah, and their sin is very great. I must go down to find out whether or not the accusations which I have heard are true.'

Then the two men left and went on towards Sodom, but the Lord remained with Abraham. Abraham approached the Lord and asked, 'Are you really going to destroy the innocent with the guilty? If there are fifty innocent people in the city, will you destroy the whole city? Won't you spare it in order to save the fifty? Surely you won't kill the innocent with the guilty. That's impossible! You can't do that. If you did, the innocent would be punished along with the guilty. That is impossible. The judge of all the earth has to act justly.'

The Lord answered, 'If I find fifty innocent people in Sodom, I will spare the whole city for their sake.'

Abraham spoke again: 'Please forgive my boldness in continuing to speak to you, Lord. I am only a man and have no right to say anything. But perhaps there will be only forty-five innocent people instead of fifty. Will you destroy the whole city because there are five too few?'

The Lord answered, 'I will not destroy the city if I find forty-five innocent people.'

Abraham spoke again: 'Perhaps there will be only forty.'

He replied, 'I will not destroy it if there are forty.'

Abraham said, 'Please don't be angry, Lord, but I must speak again. What if there are only thirty?'

He said, 'I will not do it if I find thirty.'

Abraham said, 'Please forgive my boldness in continuing to speak to you, Lord. Suppose that only twenty are found?'

He said, 'I will not destroy the city if I find twenty.'

Abraham said, 'Please don't be angry, Lord, and I will speak just once more. What if only ten are found?'

He said, 'I will not destroy it if there are ten.' After he had finished speaking with Abraham, the Lord went away, and Abraham returned home.

IT'S A DEAL!

Abraham had just had a rather unexpected visit from **three angels** and we catch up with him *again* as he prepares to send his **special guests** on their way. What Abraham *didn't* know was that meeting up with him and his wife Sarah wasn't their *only* mission.

They were *now* heading towards the cities of **Sodom** and **Gomorrah** to check out if the people there were really as **bad** as the rumours that had reached heaven.

As Abraham and the angels looked down on the valley towards these places the angels let Abraham in on what they were up to.

It didn't take Abraham long to find out that God was planning to **wipe** these cities off the **face of the earth** because the people had become so **wicked**. As two of the angels made tracks for Sodom to continue their investigations Abraham began to bargain with the one remaining angel.

Well, when I say *angel*, it could in fact have been **God** *himself* in human form because Abraham keeps calling him **Lord**.

Whatever way you look at it these men were from **heaven** and they were on a **mission from God**.

Then Abraham asked the Lord a rather tricky question . . .

ARE YOU REALLY GOING TO DESTROY THE INNOCENT WITH THE GUILTY? IF THERE ARE FIFTY INNOCENT PEOPLE IN THE CITY WILL YOU DESTROY THE WHOLE CITY?

The **Bible** says that the **Lord** answered: 'If I find **fifty** innocent people in Sodom I will spare the *whole* city.'

Seems fair to me.

'Forgive my boldness in continuing to speak to you, Lord. I am only one man and have no right to say anything. But perhaps there will be only **forty-five** innocent people instead of fifty. Will you destroy the whole city because there are five too few?' Abraham piped up.

Amazingly the Lord agreed with Abraham's bold request that if there were indeed just **forty-five** innocent people in **Sodom** then it would be spared. But Abraham didn't stop at *that*. Perhaps that's why God had handpicked him from the start – because he was a **just** and **fair** man who cared passionately about people.

Anyway, Abraham just kept on **bargaining with the Lord**.

What if there were **forty** innocent people?

How about **thirty**? **Twenty**? **Ten**?

And at ten the Lord called a halt to the negotiations and the two went their separate ways.

SODOM & GOMORRAH DESTROYED

WHAT'S IT ALL ABOUT?

This Bible story is about how God destroys the wicked cities of Sodom and Gomorrah but saves Lot and his family

WHO ARE THE MAIN CHARACTERS?

Two angels, Lot, his wife (but not for much longer) his two daughters and loads of wicked men

WHERE'S IT FOUND IN THE BIBLE?

Genesis 19:1-26

HERE'S THE BIBLE PASSAGE...

When the two angels came to Sodom that evening, Lot was sitting at the city gate. As soon as he saw them, he got up and went to meet them. He bowed down before them and said, 'Sirs, I am here to serve you. Please come to my house. You can wash your feet and stay the night. In the morning you can get up early and go on your way.'

But they answered, 'No, we will spend the night here in the city square.'

He kept on urging them, and finally they went with him to his house. Lot ordered his servants to bake some bread and prepare a fine meal for the guests. When it was ready, they ate it. Before the guests went to bed, the men of Sodom surrounded the house. All the men of the city, both young and old, were there. They called out to Lot and asked, 'Where are the men who came to stay with you tonight? Bring them out to us!' The men of Sodom wanted to have sex with them.

Lot went outside and closed the door behind him. He said to them, 'Friends, I beg you, don't do such a wicked thing! Look, I have two daughters who are still virgins. Let me bring them out to you, and you can do whatever you want with them. But don't do anything to these men; they are guests in my house, and I must protect them.'

But they said, 'Get out of our way, you foreigner! Who are you to tell us what to do? Out of our way, or we will treat you worse than them.' They pushed Lot back and moved up to break down the door. But the two men inside reached out, pulled Lot back into the house, and shut the door. Then they struck all the men outside with blindness, so that they couldn't find the door. The two men said to

Lot, 'If you have anyone else here – sons, daughters, sons-in-law, or any other relatives living in the city – get them out of here, because we are going to destroy this place. The Lord has heard the terrible accusations against these people and has sent us to destroy Sodom.'

Then Lot went to the men that his daughters were going to marry, and said, 'Hurry up and get out of here; the Lord is going to destroy this place.' But they thought he was joking. At dawn the angels tried to make Lot hurry. 'Quick!' they said. 'Take your wife and your two daughters and get out, so that you will not lose your lives when the city is destroyed.' Lot hesitated. The Lord, however, had pity on him; so the men took him, his wife, and his two daughters by the hand and led them out of the city. Then one of the angels said, 'Run for your lives! Don't look back and don't stop in the valley. Run to the hills, so that you won't be killed.' But Lot answered, 'No, please don't make us do that, sir. You have done me a great favour and saved my life. But the hills are too far away; the disaster will overtake me, and I will die before I get there. Do you see that little town? It is near enough. Let me go over there – you can see it is just a small place – and I will be safe.'

He answered, 'All right, I agree. I won't destroy that town. Hurry! Run! I can't do anything until you get there.'

Because Lot called it small, the town was named Zoar. The sun was rising when Lot reached Zoar. Suddenly the Lord rained burning sulphur on the cities of Sodom and Gomorrah and destroyed them and the whole valley, along with all the people there and everything that grew on the land. But Lot's wife looked back and was turned into a pillar of salt.

DESTRUCTION!

Lot (who is centre stage in *this* Bible bit) was the nephew of well-known Bible hero **Abraham**, so basically he had a **lot** going for him (if you'll pardon the pun!). Lot, for some unexplained reason, was sitting by the city gate in **Sodom**. Perhaps he just wanted a bit of peace and quiet. Who knows? As evening closed in **two angels** arrived.

Coincidentally they'd just come from a **dinner date** with Abraham but that's *another* story.

As they were angels, Lot did the only thing you *could* do when meeting messengers from God face to face – he **bowed down** before them.

Being a hospitable sort of chappie (like his uncle), Lot invited them back to his home for the night.

The angels declined. They were planning to spend the **night** in the **city square**. Lot didn't fancy that in the *least* and, after a considerable amount of persuasion, convinced the pair to accept his offer of a bed for the night. Back at Lot's place the angels were spoiled **something rotten** but just as they were about to turn in for the night **something rotten** *really* happened. A crowd of men from the city had surrounded Lot's house and were dead set on causing the guests **harm**. Lot was having *none* of it which only made them *angrier*. It was obvious to the angels that the people of the city were **wicked through and through**. Just as the wicked crowd were about to break down the door of Lot's house the angels pulled a master-stroke . . . they struck the crowd of men **blind**. It was now or never to escape.

The angels gave Lot his instructions . . .

GET ALL YOUR RELATIVES QUICKLY. THE LORD IS GOING TO DESTROY THIS TERRIBLE AND WICKED CITY!

The trouble was that *everybody* thought that Lot was **joking** when he urged them to **run for their lives**. They'd probably got so *used* to the wickedness that they couldn't imagine for one *moment* that God would want to **destroy them**. It was *only* because the two angels grabbed them by the hand that Lot's wife and two daughters escaped. If they'd had *their* way they'd have probably stayed put.

Lot, his family and the angels raced away from Sodom as far as they could run. Poor Lot was so exhausted the angels agreed to let him stop at a place could **Zoar** which they reached just as the sun was rising.

Suddenly **burning sulphur** rained down from the sky and destroyed the cities of Sodom and Gomorrah.

The Bible says that Lot's wife looked back and was turned into a **pillar of salt** (because salt was also raining down).

How did *that* happen? Perhaps it meant she actually turned back and *returned* to those wicked cities rather than go with **God**, and that's how she got destroyed.

You'll have to work *that* one out yourself!

ABRAHAM AND ABIMELECH

WHAT'S IT ALL ABOUT?

This Bible story is about how Abraham pretended that his wife Sarah was his sister to protect himself (from being killed)

WHO ARE THE MAIN CHARACTERS?

Abraham, Sarah and poor unfortunate King Abimelech

WHERE'S IT FOUND IN THE BIBLE?

Genesis 20:1-18

HERE'S THE BIBLE PASSAGE...

Abraham moved from Mamre to the southern part of Canaan and lived between Kadesh and Shur. Later, while he was living in Gerar, he said that his wife Sarah was his sister. So King Abimelech of Gerar had Sarah brought to him. One night God appeared to him in a dream and said: 'You are going to die, because you have taken this woman; she is already married.'

But Abimelech had not come near her, and he said, 'Lord, I am innocent! Would you destroy me and my people? Abraham himself said that she was his sister, and she said the same thing. I did this with a clear conscience, and I have done no wrong.'

God replied in the dream, 'Yes, I know that you did it with a clear conscience; so I kept you from sinning against me and did not let you touch her. But now, give the woman back to her husband. He is a prophet, and he will pray for you, so that you will not die. But if you do not give her back, I warn you that you are going to die, you and all your people.'

Early the next morning Abimelech called all his officials and told them what had happened, and they were terrified. Then Abimelech called Abraham and asked, 'What have you done to us? What wrong have I done to you to make you bring this disaster on me and my kingdom? No one should ever do what you have done to me. Why did you do it?'

Abraham answered, 'I thought that there would be no one here who has reverence for God and that they would kill me to get my wife. She really is my sister. She is the daughter of my father, but not of my mother, and I married her. So when God sent me from my father's house into foreign lands, I said to her, "You can show how loyal you are to me by telling everyone that I am your brother."'

Then Abimelech gave Sarah back to Abraham, and at the same time he gave him sheep, cattle, and slaves. He said to Abraham, 'Here is my whole land; live anywhere you like.' He said to Sarah, 'I am giving your brother a thousand pieces of silver as proof to all who are with you that you are innocent; everyone will know that you have done no wrong.'

Because of what had happened to Sarah, Abraham's wife, the Lord had made it impossible for any woman in Abimelech's palace to have children. So Abraham prayed for Abimelech, and God healed him. He also healed his wife and his slave women, so that they could have children.

SISTER ACT!

There's *heaps* of stuff about **Abraham** in the Bible and *here's* a tale about him that's packed with fear and deception (thought *that* would appeal to you).

Abraham was on a bit of a camping tour of **Southern Canaan** (that's the advantage of living in a tent, I suppose) and had stopped off in **Gerar** where, as far as Abraham knew, nobody cared the *least* bit about **God** or for that matter anybody who *served* God – such as Abraham. **King Abimelech of Gerar** took a shine to Abraham's wife Sarah (even though she was **90 years old**!?) so he took her back to his palace or wherever the king of Gerar lived. Abraham had told the king that Sarah was his **sister**, which was true in a *roundabout* sort of way but not the *complete* truth.

They both had the same dad but a *different* mother so to be strictly accurate Sarah was actually Abraham's **half-sister**. Why was Abraham so economical with the truth? Simple.

He was **scared silly** that if King Abimelech thought Sarah was his wife he'd have Abraham bumped off (killed) and make Sarah *his* wife instead.

I THOUGHT THAT BECAUSE SHE WAS MY HALF-SISTER I COULD GET AWAY WITH A HALF-TRUTH. OBVIOUSLY NOT!

Before the unsuspecting king even had the *chance* to get to know Sarah better, he had an unexpected (and rather *scary*) dream from **God**. God told King Abimelech in no uncertain terms to keep his **hands off** Sarah because she was married to *his* man, Abraham.

Poor Abimelech pleaded his innocence with God who accepted what he said as the truth.

But the point was that even if Sarah *hadn't* been Abraham's wife, taking *anything* from a man of God like Abraham, was a **big mistake**.

It was as if God was saying, 'You mess with **Abraham** then you mess with **me**!'

At the **crack of dawn** the next day the king set about getting things straight with Abraham.

God had told him that Abraham was going to have to pray for him so that he wouldn't die.

It wasn't only *Abimelech* who was **terrified** of getting on the **wrong side of God** – all his *officials* were!

Such was the **seriousness** of messing with **God's man** that even the women of the land had been prevented from having children as a **punishment**.

Abraham prayed for Abimelech and everything was sorted. **Phew!** *That* was a close one for the king.

And just to make *sure* Abraham (and God) understood how truly sorry he was, the king sent Abraham and his entourage off with **heaps of goodies** (sheep, cattle, slaves and silver).

THE BIRTH OF ISAAC

WHAT'S IT ALL ABOUT?

This Bible story is about the birth of God's promised son (Isaac) to Abraham and Sarah

WHO ARE THE MAIN CHARACTERS?

Abraham, Sarah and of course Isaac

WHERE'S IT FOUND IN THE BIBLE?

Genesis 21:1-8

HERE'S THE BIBLE PASSAGE...

The Lord blessed Sarah, as he had promised, and she became pregnant and bore a son to Abraham when he was old. The boy was born at the time God had said he would be born. Abraham named him Isaac, and when Isaac was eight days old, Abraham circumcised him, as God had commanded. Abraham was a hundred years old when Isaac was born. Sarah said, 'God has brought me joy and laughter. Everyone who hears about it will laugh with me.' Then she added, 'Who would have said to Abraham that Sarah would nurse children? Yet I have borne him a son in his old age.' The child grew, and on the day that he was weaned, Abraham gave a great feast.

BOY-OH-BOY!

This Bible bit is probably one of the **shortest** we've got for you but it's probably one of the most **important** ones. 'Why's *that*?' you may ask. Well, even if you *didn't* ask I'm still going to tell you.

Abraham (if you didn't know already) had been handpicked by **God** to head up a brand-new nation of people who were totally sold out for God. Most people weren't the *least* bit interested in being friends with the God who'd created the whole whopping great universe and, for that matter, **them**.

Which is a bit of a *shame* really 'cos that's the whole *purpose* of God making us in the *first* place.

Anyway, on with the story.

To start up a brand-new nation there was one thing Abraham needed which (until now) he didn't have ... **descendants**.

And to have descendants it would be really handy if he had a son to get the thing up and running. (Well, actually it was *essential*!)

Although Abraham and his wife **Sarah** were **over the hill** when it came to having kids, God always likes to have the *last* laugh, which in *this* case was helping Sarah to fall pregnant at the extremely ripe old age of ninety. (Ripe? Perhaps **over-ripe** be might be a *better* description.)

Just like God had *promised*, Sarah gave birth to a **son** (and exactly when God had *said* she would).

Abraham called the lad **Isaac** (*also* like God had told them) and when he was eight days old Abraham circumcised him. (A special itsy-bitsy operation for boys to show they belonged to God.)

It was a **double celebration** in their household that year because Abraham had hit a **hundred**.

Now that's what I *call* a **generation gap**!

Sarah was thrilled to bits to be a mum after the short matter of a **ninety-year wait**.

'God has brought me joy and laughter. Everyone who hears about it will laugh with me,' she said.

Too right!

Sarah wasn't the *only* one to have laughed at the thought of a baby being born to ancient parents – Abraham had. Which is why it won't surprise you to learn that Isaac actually means **'he laughs'**.

How appropriate!

The Bible says that Abraham celebrated the birth of Isaac with a great feast. (And probably a quiet snooze later – you know what these old folks are like!)

ABRAHAM IS TESTED BY GOD

WHAT'S IT ALL ABOUT?

This Bible story is about how God tested Abraham as to how much confidence he had in him

WHO ARE THE MAIN CHARACTERS?

Abraham, Isaac and an angel are the main ones but also two servants, a donkey and a ram with very bad timing

WHERE'S IT FOUND IN THE BIBLE?

Genesis 22:1-19

HERE'S THE BIBLE PASSAGE...

Some time later God tested Abraham; he called to him, 'Abraham!' And Abraham answered, 'Yes, here I am!'

'Take your son,' God said, 'your only son, Isaac, whom you love so much, and go to the land of Moriah. There on a mountain that I will show you, offer him as a sacrifice to me.'

Early the next morning Abraham cut some wood for the sacrifice, loaded his donkey, and took Isaac and two servants with him. They started out for the place that God had told him about. On the third day Abraham saw the place in the distance. Then he said to the servants, 'Stay here with the donkey. The boy and I will go over there and worship, and then we will come back to you.' Abraham made Isaac carry the wood for the sacrifice, and he himself carried a knife and live coals for starting the fire.

As they walked along together, Isaac said, 'Father!'

He answered, 'Yes, my son?'

Isaac asked, 'I see that you have the coals and the wood, but where is the lamb for the sacrifice?'

Abraham answered, 'God himself will provide one.' And the two of them walked on together. When they came to the place which God had told him about, Abraham built an altar and arranged the wood on it. He tied up his son and placed him on the altar, on top of the wood. Then he picked up the knife to kill him. But the angel of the Lord called to him from heaven, 'Abraham, Abraham!'

He answered, 'Yes, here I am.'

'Don't hurt the boy or do anything to him,' he said. 'Now I know that you honour and obey God, because you have not kept back your only son from him.'

Abraham looked round and saw a ram caught in a bush by its horns. He went and got it and offered it as a burnt offering instead of his son. Abraham named that place 'The Lord Provides'. And even today people say, 'On the Lord's mountain he provides.'

The angel of the Lord called to Abraham from heaven a second time, 'I make a vow by my own name – the Lord is speaking – that I will richly bless you. Because you did this and did not keep back your only son from me, I promise that I will give you as many descendants as there are stars in the sky or grains of sand along the seashore. Your descendants will conquer their enemies. All the nations will ask me to bless them as I have blessed your descendants – all because you obeyed my command.'

Abraham went back to his servants, and they went together to Beersheba, where Abraham settled.

BARBECUE TIME!

How do you feel when your mum or dad tells you to **share something** with your brother or sister.

Unless they've picked a *good* day then giving it up doesn't come easy. **Abraham** is about to be asked by **God** to give up more than just the **Gameboy** or the **TV remote** for half an hour.

Let's catch up with him and find out what's going on.

Abraham had just had a message from God that would make the hairs on *most* people's necks stand up.

God wanted **Abraham** to take his son (**Isaac**) to the land of Moriah and **sacrifice him to God**.

Just in case you're not *completely* sure what a sacrifice is in the Bible, well it generally involves killing something and then burning it up to please God.

The thing is, Abraham didn't even *argue* with God.

He just cut some wood, loaded his donkey, collared a couple of his servants and first thing next morning set off to obey God (with Isaac as well, of course!).

If you know *anything* about Abraham you'll know that he'd waited *years* to have a son and *now* it looked like God was going to **take him** from him.

Not only *that* but God had promised Abraham that *through* Isaac, he would have **countless descendants**. This thing just *didn't* seem to add up but there was one thing that Abraham was *definitely* famous for – **trusting God**.

After **three days of trekking** they arrived at the mountain God had told Abraham to sacrifice Isaac on. Leaving his servants to tend the donkey, Abraham set out with his son . . .

Hmm, well it would seem that nobody had let *Isaac* in on the plan yet!

When they finally arrived at the place appointed by God, Abraham set about building a **stone altar** to burn his sacrifice on. After carefully arranging the wood around it he **placed Isaac on it**.

Makes you wonder what was going through *both* of their minds, doesn't it?

Do you think Isaac *really* thought his own dad would carry it through?

And what must *Abraham* have felt having to give up his son and heir? The time for talking is up.

Abraham raised his knife to kill Isaac but as he did so, an **angel** called out from heaven *not* to harm the lad. **Gulp!** *That* was a close one!

'Now I know you honour and obey God and have not kept back your only son from him,' said the angel. Abraham spotted a **ram** caught in a bush and sacrificed it *instead*. (Bad luck, ram!)

Because Abraham had been prepared to give up even his *son* to God, *God* in turn promised Abraham that he wouldn't hold back from giving him **absolutely anything** . . .

ISAAC AND REBECCA

WHAT'S IT ALL ABOUT?

This Bible story is about Abraham's search for a bride for his son Isaac

WHO ARE THE MAIN CHARACTERS?

Abraham, his trusty servant and Rebecca. Bit parts are played by numerous camels

WHERE'S IT FOUND IN THE BIBLE?

Genesis 24:1-28

HERE'S THE BIBLE PASSAGE...

Abraham was now very old, and the Lord had blessed him in everything he did. He said to his oldest servant, who was in charge of all that he had, 'Place your hand between my thighs and make a vow. I want you to make a vow in the name of the Lord, the God of heaven and earth, that you will not choose a wife for my son from the people here in Canaan. You must go back to the country where I was born and get a wife for my son Isaac from among my relatives.'

But the servant asked, 'What if the young woman will not leave home to come with me to this land? Shall I send your son back to the land you came from?'

Abraham answered, 'Make sure that you don't send my son back there! The Lord, the God of heaven, brought me from the home of my father and from the land of my relatives, and he solemnly promised me that he would give this land to my descendants. He will send his angel before you, so that you can get a wife there for my son. If the young woman is not willing to come with you, you will be free from this promise. But you must not under any circumstances take my son back there.' So the servant put his hand between the thighs of Abraham, his master, and made a vow to do what Abraham had asked.

The servant, who was in charge of Abraham's property, took ten of his master's camels and went to the city where Nahor had lived in northern Mesopotamia. When he arrived, he made the camels kneel down at the well outside the city. It was late afternoon, the time when women came out to get water. He prayed, 'Lord, God of my master Abraham, give me success today and keep your promise to my master. Here I am at the well where the young women of the city will be coming to get water. I will say to one of them, "Please, lower your jar and let me have a drink." If she says, "Drink, and I will also bring water for your camels", may she be the one that you have chosen for your servant Isaac. If this happens, I will know that you have kept your promise to my master.'

Before he had finished praying, Rebecca arrived with a water jar on her shoulder. She was the daughter of Bethuel, who was the son of Abraham's brother Nahor and his wife Milcah. She was a very beautiful young woman and still a virgin. She went down to the well, filled her jar, and came back. The servant ran to meet her and said, 'Please give me a drink of water from your jar.'

She said, 'Drink, sir,' and quickly lowered her jar from her shoulder and held it while he drank. When he had finished, she said, 'I will also bring water for your camels and let them have all they want.' She quickly emptied her jar into the animals' drinking-trough and ran to the well to get more water, until she had watered all his camels. The man kept watching her in silence, to see if the Lord had given him success.

When she had finished, the man took an expensive gold ring and put it in her nose and put two large gold bracelets on her arms. He said, 'Please tell me who your father is. Is there room in his house for my men and me to spend the night?'

'My father is Bethuel, son of Nahor and Milcah,' she answered. 'There is plenty of straw and fodder at our house, and there is a place for you to stay.' Then the man knelt down and worshipped the Lord. He said, 'Praise the Lord, the God of my master Abraham, who has faithfully kept his promise to my master. The Lord has led me straight to my master's relatives.' The young woman ran to her mother's house and told the whole story.

BLIND DATE!

This Bible story is all about getting Abraham's son **Isaac** hitched up with a wife. **Abraham** was a very old man but before he popped his clogs (died) he wanted to make sure Isaac was married off.

And Abraham *didn't* want Isaac having *any* old wife. Isaac's wife had to be someone who worshipped the *same* **God** that *he* did but *that* meant heading back to where most of Abraham's family still lived (in Mesopotamia) – **hundreds of miles away**. Abraham couldn't do a journey like that at his age and there was no way that *Isaac* was gonna leave the **land of Canaan** which God had told them to live in. In fact Abraham made the servant promise *not* to take Isaac back to **Mesopotamia**.

There was nothing for it but for Abraham's oldest (and most trustworthy) servant to go and find Isaac a bride. Along with **ten camels** the servant set out on the long journey. There's one thing camels need after a long trek and that's **a nice cool drink**. Which is why the servant made a beeline for the well outside the city. If this mission was going to be a *success* then the servant figured that it was now time to get **God** in on the thing. So he set about **praying** . . .

LORD, GOD OF MY MASTER ABRAHAM, GIVE ME SUCCESS TODAY. HERE I AM AT THE WELL WHERE THE YOUNG WOMEN OF THE CITY WILL BE COMING TO GET WATER. I WILL SAY TO ONE OF THEM, 'PLEASE LOWER YOUR JAR AND LET ME HAVE A DRINK', AND IF SHE SAYS, 'DRINK, AND I WILL ALSO BRING WATER FOR YOUR CAMELS', MAY SHE BE THE ONE THAT YOU HAVE CHOSEN FOR YOUR SERVANT ISAAC.

Before he'd even *finished* praying a young woman called **Rebecca** arrived to fill her water jar.

When the servant asked her for a drink of water Rebecca replied *just* like the servant had prayed she would.

The servant **couldn't believe it**.

He'd got the **bullseye** first time – all thanks to God.

As soon as Rebecca had finished watering the camels he took an expensive gold ring and put it through her nose (I presume there was a hole there already!) and put two large gold bracelets on her arm. The servant was positively **itching** to find out who her **father** was, and when he discovered it was a chap called **Bethuel** who was actually *related* to Abraham he was **over the moon**.

Abraham's servant fell down on his knees and worshipped God – but then what *else* could you do after such an **amazing event** like that?

THE BIRTH OF ESAU AND JACOB

WHAT'S IT ALL ABOUT?

This Bible story is about the rather unusual circumstance of the birth of Esau and Jacob

WHO ARE THE MAIN CHARACTERS?

Rebecca (the mum) and her twin boys, Esau and Jacob

WHERE'S IT FOUND IN THE BIBLE?

Genesis 25:19-26

HERE'S THE BIBLE PASSAGE...

This is the story of Abraham's son Isaac. Isaac was 40 years old when he married Rebecca, the daughter of Bethuel (an Aramean from Mesopotamia) and sister of Laban. Because Rebecca had no children, Isaac prayed to the Lord for her. The Lord answered his prayer, and Rebecca became pregnant. She was going to have twins, and before they were born, they struggled against each other in her womb. She said, 'Why should something like this happen to me?' So she went to ask the Lord for an answer.

The Lord said to her:
'Two nations are within you. You will give birth to two rival peoples.
'One will be stronger than the other.
'The older will serve the younger.'
The time came for her to give birth, and she had twin sons. The first one was reddish, and his skin was like a hairy robe, so he was named Esau. The second one was born holding on tightly to the heel of Esau, so he was named Jacob. Isaac was 60 years old when they were born.

BATTLING BABIES!

This Bible bit is all about a guy called **Isaac** and his new wife, **Rebecca**. One thing the Bible kindly tells us is that Isaac was **40 years old** when he got hitched to Beccy (sorry, *Rebecca*) but seeing as ladies aren't too fond of having their age broadcast to the world at large, the Bible remains **silent** on how long *she'd* been around. Never mind! One thing the Bible *does* tell us is that Isaac's good lady wife seemed to be having a bit of trouble falling pregnant. Now *there's* a coincidence because that's the *same* problem Isaac's **mum** had (but not for *too* long otherwise there wouldn't be any Isaac, would there?). Not having any kids was a little bit awkward for our Isaac 'cos God had already told him that his descendants would grow into a **whopping big nation**. There was nothing for it!

Isaac did what every sensible person does when they're in a fix – **he prayed to God**.

The *good news* is that **God** heard Isaac's prayer and before you could say, '**You've gotta be kidding!**', Rebecca was pregnant.

Hang on a minute! Why would someone want to say, 'You've gotta be kidding!', when they'd just had their prayer miraculously answered? *Here's* why.

Rebecca was going to give birth to **twins** . . . and **twin boys** at that!

God hadn't just given them *one* child – he dolloped *two* on them. Now isn't that **generous** of God.

But then again, generosity is something God's good at.

But having twins wasn't *all* sweetness and light. **No way!**

Even *before* they'd popped out of Rebecca's tummy (well, *womb* if you want to be picky) they started to **struggle** against each other. Let's be honest, having a couple of **bickering kids** inside you can't be much fun, which is why Rebecca decided to have it out with God . . .

A very good question, Rebecca! And *this* was God's reply:

'Two nations are within you. You will give birth to two rival peoples. One will be stronger than the other. The older will serve the younger.'

Hmm! It seems like Isaac and Rebecca's kids were destined for more than the *usual* Middle Eastern upbringing. But perhaps we'll find out more of that *another* time.

But for *now*, all you need to know is that in due time the **battling boys** were born and they were named **Esau** and **Jacob**. It wasn't much of a good start for poor Esau. The Bible tells us that he had **reddish skin** and was like a **hairy robe**. (Ugh!!) The Bible *also* tells us that Jacob was grabbing on to Esau's heel as he entered the big, wide world. Looks like the battle is on between these two, doesn't it?

ESAU SELLS HIS BIRTHRIGHT

WHAT'S IT ALL ABOUT?

This Bible story is about Esau and Jacob and how Jacob tricked Esau out of his birthright

WHO ARE THE MAIN CHARACTERS?

Jacob and Esau are out centre stage but their parents, Isaac and Rebecca, get a mention

WHERE'S IT FOUND IN THE BIBLE?

Genesis 25:27-34

HERE'S THE BIBLE PASSAGE...

The boys grew up, and Esau became a skilled hunter, a man who loved the outdoor life, but Jacob was a quiet man who stayed at home. Isaac preferred Esau, because he enjoyed eating the animals Esau killed, but Rebecca preferred Jacob.

One day while Jacob was cooking some bean soup, Esau came in from hunting. He was hungry and said to Jacob, 'I'm starving; give me some of that red stuff.' (That is why he was called Edom.*)

Jacob answered, 'I will give it to you if you give me your rights as the firstborn son.' Esau said, 'All right! I am about to die; what good will my rights do me then?'

Jacob answered, 'First make a vow that you will give me your rights.'

Esau made the vow and gave his rights to Jacob. Then Jacob gave him some bread and some of the soup. He ate and drank and then got up and left. That was all Esau cared about his rights as the firstborn son.

*This name sounds like Hebrew for 'red'.

DOUBLE TROUBLE!

If you've got a brother then this story's *definitely* one for **you**! What we've got here is **Jacob** and **Esau** (twin brothers) who, to put it bluntly, didn't really hit it off.

Esau was more the **rough, tough, outdoor type** while **Jacob** just preferred to **stay at home** with his mummy (being the quiet chap that he was). And nothing wrong with *that*, I say!

While Jacob was doing whatever quiet, indoor-type people did in those days, Esau was roaming the country-side killing animals – and very good at it he was *too*, well at least so the *Bible* tells us.

Isaac (their dad) was rather partial to tucking into a juicy bit of meat so Esau was *his* favourite.

Rebecca, on the other hand, had a soft spot for her home-loving son, Jacob. Perhaps because he spent more time helping round the house? Who knows, but that's where we catch up with Jacob at the start of this story. In fact, Jacob wasn't just helping out with the odd bit of dusting and house cleaning. Nope! Not *this* particular day, anyway. Our Jacob was cooking up a **scrummy bean soup**, no less (yum!).

But guess who should charge through the kitchen door at that moment?

Red stuff? How rude! I'll have you know that Jacob's bean soup is very highly thought of, thank you very much.

But Jacob didn't seem too miffed by Esau's unkind description of his food – he was probably used to it. Anyway, the long and the short of it was that Esau agreed to Jacob's **ridiculous suggestion**.

I mean, imagine trading *everything* that your dad was going to leave you when he died all for the sake of a plate of '**red stuff**'? oops, sorry – **bean soup**.

Jacob might have been the quiet one but he was certainly the more *devious* of the two. He got Esau to make a vow (which is like an absolutely **100 per cent unbreakable promise**) that he'd keep to *his* side of the bargain and hand over to Jacob all his **rights** of being the eldest son.

And after scoffing down his rather expensive plate of red stuff (I mean **bean soup**) he stormed off.

The Bible tells us that Esau didn't care **two hoots** for his birthright (though it puts it a bit *nicer* than that!).

That's it for *this* story but keep an eye out for those **terrible twins** – there's more double trouble where *that* came from!

ISAAC BLESSES JACOB

WHAT'S IT ALL ABOUT?

This Bible story is about Jacob tricking his dad (Isaac) into giving him his blessing rather than to the eldest son, Esau

WHO ARE THE MAIN CHARACTERS?

Rebecca and Jacob pit themselves against Isaac and Esau

WHERE'S IT FOUND IN THE BIBLE?

Genesis 27:1-35

HERE'S THE BIBLE PASSAGE...

Isaac was now old and had become blind. He sent for his elder son Esau and said to him, 'My son!'

'Yes,' he answered.

Isaac said, 'You see that I am old and may die soon. Take your bow and arrows, go out into the country, and kill an animal for me. Cook me some of that tasty food that I like, and bring it to me. After I have eaten it, I will give you my final blessing before I die.'

While Isaac was talking to Esau, Rebecca was listening. So when Esau went out to hunt, she said to Jacob, 'I have just heard your father say to Esau, "Bring me an animal and cook it for me. After I have eaten it, I will give you my blessing in the presence of the Lord before I die." Now, my son,' Rebecca continued, 'listen to me and do what I say. Go to the flock and pick out two fat young goats, so that I can cook them and make some of that food your father likes so much. You can take it to him to eat, and he will give you his blessing before he dies.'

But Jacob said to his mother, 'You know that Esau is a hairy man, but I have smooth skin. Perhaps my father will touch me and find out that I am deceiving him; in this way I will bring a curse on myself instead of a blessing.'

His mother answered, 'Let any curse against you fall on me, my son; just do as I say, and go and get the goats for me.' So he went to get them and brought them to her, and she cooked the kind of food that his father liked. Then she took Esau's best clothes, which she kept in the house, and put them on Jacob. She put the skins of the goats on his arms and on the hairless part of his neck. She handed him the tasty food, together with the bread she had baked.

Then Jacob went to his father and said, 'Father!'

'Yes,' he answered. 'Which of my sons are you?'

Jacob answered, 'I am your elder son Esau; I have done as you told me. Please sit up and eat some of the meat that I have brought you, so that you can give me your blessing.'

Isaac said, 'How did you find it so quickly, my son?'

Jacob answered, 'The Lord your God helped me to find it.'

Isaac said to Jacob, 'Please come closer so that I can touch you. Are you really Esau?' Jacob moved closer to his father, who felt him and said, 'Your voice sounds like Jacob's voice, but your arms feel like Esau's arms.' He did not recognise Jacob, because his arms were hairy like Esau's. He was about to give him his blessing, but asked again, 'Are you really Esau?'

'I am,' he answered.

Isaac said, 'Bring me some of the meat. After I have eaten it, I will give you my blessing.' Jacob brought it to him, and he also brought him some wine to drink. Then his father said to him, 'Come closer and kiss me, my son.' As he came up to kiss him, Isaac smelt his clothes, so he gave him his blessing. He said, 'The pleasant smell of my son is like the smell of a field which the Lord has blessed. May God give you dew from heaven and make your fields fertile! May he give you plenty of corn and wine! May nations be your servants, and may peoples bow down before you. May you rule over all your relatives, and may your mother's descendants bow down before you. May those who curse you be cursed, and may those who bless you be blessed.' Isaac finished giving his blessing, and as soon as Jacob left, his brother Esau came in from hunting. He also cooked some tasty food and took it to his father. He said, 'Please, father, sit up and eat some of the meat that I have brought you, so that you can give me your blessing.'

'Who are you?' Isaac asked.

'Your elder son, Esau,' he answered. Isaac began to tremble and shake all over, and he asked, 'Who was it, then, who killed an animal and brought it to me? I ate it just before you came. I gave him my final blessing, and so it is his for ever.' When Esau heard this, he cried out loudly and bitterly and said, 'Give me your blessing also, father!'

Isaac answered, 'Your brother came and deceived me. He has taken away your blessing.'

TRICKED AND TREAT!

What's the **biggest mistake** a parent can make when they've got more than one kid? Simple!

It's having a **favourite**. But I can only guess that nobody ever bothered to let **Isaac** and **Rebecca** in on that useful bit of info. *Their* twin boys, **Esau** and **Jacob** were *forever* at each other's throats and to make matters *worse* Isaac seemed to hit it off better with **rough, tough** Esau while Rebecca had a bit of a soft spot for **home-loving** Jacob.

We catch up with them just as Isaac is about to give his **blessing** to Esau (the eldest son). Isaac reckons he's on his deathbed so there's no time to waste. If you think that getting your dad's blessing is no big deal then *think again*. Whichever of these two boys gets the blessing gets **God's seal of approval** for the rest of their life. That's why, when Rebecca overheard Isaac telling Esau to go get him something to eat and then he'd bless him, his conniving wife hatched her *own* **cunning plan**.

While Esau headed out into the open countryside to catch a tasty animal to cook, Rebecca was eyeing up a tasty meal closer to home. Nabbing Jacob, she packed him off in the direction of their nearby flock of goats. There was no way that *Esau* was going to have that blessing if *she* had anything to do with it.

In no time at all, Jacob's mum had knocked up a **scrummy meal** for Isaac.

Now all *Jacob* had to do was convince his dad that *he* was his **hairy brother**. Rebecca had already thought of that. First off she dressed Jacob in some of Esau's clothes, then she covered his arms and neck with **goat skins** to make him feel hairy to the touch. OK, so Jacob might have *looked* ridiculous but one thing I forgot to tell you was that Isaac was almost **blind**. He wouldn't have any *idea* that the man in **fancy dress** *wasn't* his beloved **Esau** but in fact **Jacob**.

Time to put the plan into action. Would Isaac suspect anything?

To Jacob's relief, his dad fell for his trickery, hook, line and sinker and after Isaac had gobbled up his delicious dinner he gave Jacob his blessing.

When Esau eventually returned from his hunting expedition (and after cooking up a rather nice plate of grub) he headed off to **get his blessing**. It didn't take long for both Isaac and Esau to realise that they'd been well and truly **stitched up** by Jacob (and Rebecca) but there was absolutely nothing anyone could *do* about it. There was only *one* blessing on offer and *Jacob* had nabbed it. The Bible says that Esau wept bitterly. And wouldn't you? And that, as they say, was that!

JACOB'S DREAM

WHAT'S IT ALL ABOUT?

This Bible story is about how Jacob does a runner and has an angelic vision along the way

WHO ARE THE MAIN CHARACTERS?

Jacob, a stairway-full of angels and a lump of rock (a.k.a. his pillow)

WHERE'S IT FOUND IN THE BIBLE?

Genesis 28:10-22

HERE'S THE BIBLE PASSAGE...

Jacob left Beersheba and started towards Haran. At sunset he came to a holy place and camped there. He lay down to sleep, resting his head on a stone. He dreamt that he saw a stairway reaching from earth to heaven, with angels going up and coming down on it. And there was the Lord standing beside him. 'I am the Lord, the God of Abraham and Isaac,' he said. 'I will give to you and to your descendants this land on which you are lying. They will be as numerous as the specks of dust on the earth. They will extend their territory in all directions, and through you and your descendants I will bless all the nations. Remember, I will be with you and protect you wherever you go, and I will bring you back to this land. I will not leave you until I have done all that I have promised you.'

Jacob woke up and said, 'The Lord is here! He is in this place, and I didn't know it!' He was afraid and said, 'What a terrifying place this is! It must be the house of God; it must be the gate that opens into heaven.'

Jacob got up early next morning, took the stone that was under his head, and set it up as a memorial. Then he poured olive oil on it to dedicate it to God. He named the place Bethel. (The town there was once known as Luz.) Then Jacob made a vow to the Lord: 'If you will be with me and protect me on the journey I am making and give me food and clothing, and if I return safely to my father's home, then you will be my God. This memorial stone which I have set up will be the place where you are worshipped, and I will give you a tenth of everything you give me.'

ZZZZZZZZZZ!

Jacob had done a runner. He'd tricked his elder brother **Esau** out of his inheritance and was now **fleeing for his life**. He was speeding as fast as his deceiving legs could carry him in the direction of his mum's brother, **Laban**. It was a fair old hike to Haran but Jacob's mum Rebbecca figured that 'out of sight – out of mind' was the *best* way of avoiding Esau's **dastardly revenge**.

There weren't *too many* motels along the way from Beersheba to Haran (none, in fact) so, if you wanted to **kip** then your *best* bet was to grab yourself a **handy boulder** and use it as a pillow.

(Sounds a bit uncomfortable to me.)

The Bible tells us that, one night, as the sun was setting, Jacob turned in for the night (with his rocky pillow) and nodded off to sleep. Most people have pretty average dreams such as **being chased by a giant cabbage** or imagining that they're about to miss an **open goal** in the last minute of extra time at the World Cup final. Not *Jacob*. (OK, so I know football hadn't been invented then but you know what I mean.) As he drifted off into the land of nod he dreamt that he saw **loads of angels** going up and down a **stairway** that reached down from heaven to earth. *Next* he saw God who had a few things he wanted to say to our main man . . .

I AM THE LORD YOUR GOD, THE GOD OF ABRAHAM AND ISAAC. I WILL GIVE TO YOU AND YOUR DESCENDANTS THIS LAND ON WHICH YOU ARE LYING. THEY WILL BE AS NUMEROUS AS THE SPECKS OF DUST ON THE EARTH . . . I WILL PROTECT YOU WHEREVER YOU GO AND I WILL BRING YOU BACK TO THIS LAND.

Jacob woke up with a start. He was *well*-shocked. What a dream and a half *that* had been. Jacob realised that the place he'd been sleeping was something **special to God** so, at the crack of dawn, he took his pillow – I mean, **stone**, and placed it on the ground as a sort of memorial to what he'd seen in his dream.

Then Jacob **dolloped olive oil** all over the rock as a way of saying that he was **dedicating it to God**.

(And I suppose nobody *else* would be wanting to put their head on that oily pillow from now on!)

Finally, to finish things off, Jacob renamed the place (it *was* called Luz) and called it **Bethel** (which happens to mean '**House of God**', if you're interested).

I hope the *locals* didn't mind, that's all *I* can say. Just think of all those maps they'd have to change.

Before Jacob set off again for Haran, Jacob returned the compliment and made a promise to **God** that he would always worship him (*and* give God a tenth of everything that *he* gave to Jacob).

I wonder what Jacob dreamed about the *next* night. Probably **giant cabbages**, eh?

JACOB ARRIVES AT LABAN'S

WHAT'S IT ALL ABOUT?

This Bible story is about Jacob's arrival at the home of his uncle Laban (and his first glimpse of his future wife)

WHO ARE THE MAIN CHARACTERS?

Jacob, Rachel and Laban headline but there is also a large cast of sheep or goats (or both)

WHERE'S IT FOUND IN THE BIBLE?

Genesis 29:1-14

HERE'S THE BIBLE PASSAGE...

Jacob continued on his way and went towards the land of the East. Suddenly he came upon a well out in the fields with three flocks of sheep lying round it. The flocks were watered from this well, which had a large stone over the opening.

Whenever all the flocks came together there, the shepherds would roll the stone back and water them. Then they would put the stone back in place.

Jacob asked the shepherds, 'My friends, where are you from?'

'From Haran,' they answered.

He asked, 'Do you know Laban, grandson of Nahor?'

'Yes, we do,' they answered.

'Is he well?' he asked.

'He is well,' they answered. 'Look, here comes his daughter Rachel with his flock.'

Jacob said, 'Since it is still broad daylight and not yet time to bring the flocks in, why don't you water them and take them back to pasture?'

They answered, 'We can't do that until all the flocks are here and the stone has been rolled back; then we will water the flocks.'

While Jacob was still talking to them, Rachel arrived with the flock. When Jacob saw Rachel with his uncle Laban's flock, he went to the well, rolled the stone back, and watered the sheep. Then he kissed her and began to cry for joy. He told her, 'I am your father's relative, the son of Rebecca.'

She ran to tell her father; and when he heard the news about his nephew Jacob, he ran to meet him, hugged him and kissed him, and brought him into the house. When Jacob told Laban everything that had happened, Laban said, 'Yes, indeed, you are my own flesh and blood.' Jacob stayed there a whole month.

WELL, WELL, WELL!

The fella who stars in *this* Bible bit crops up quite a lot. His name is **Jacob** and he's making for his **Uncle Laban's** house where he's hoping to hide away from his **angry brother Esau**. (They've had a bit of a bust-up, OK?) After trekking for many days Jacob stumbles across a **well** (not *literally*) in the middle of a field.

Nothing unusual about *that* you say – and you'd be right! But what Jacob *didn't* know was that he was about to bump into (not *literally*) someone who was going to change his life for ever. The well in question was used by the local shepherds to water their sheep (not *literally*) – it means to give them a drink, not like watering a plant. That would be daft, wouldn't it?

According to the **Bible**, the well was *only* opened up once all the flocks had arrived, so when Jacob hit the place (not *literally*) the shepherds were still waiting for the *rest* of the flocks to show up. Being the upfront sort of guy that he was, Jacob went up to the shepherds and struck up a conversation with them . . .

Jacob couldn't believe his luck (not that he actually *believed* in luck 'cos he **trusted in God** but you know what I mean!). He'd stumbled (not *literally*) across the **very well** that his *Uncle Laban* used. God must have had more than a thing or two to do with *this*. Taking things into his own hands, Jacob rolled the stone off the well (the stone kept the well water from getting dirty) and wasted no time in proving what a good relative he was by watering (not *literally*) the flocks that **Rachel** had brought to the well.

I reckon Jacob must have been a bit of a **softy** 'cos the Bible says that he was so **overcome with joy** at seeing Rachel that he **wept** (and nothing wrong with that, *I* say!).

Jacob wasn't the *only* one to get a bit over-emotional.

Rachel rushed back home to tell her dad (**Laban**) about Jacob and when they met up Laban was all **hugs and kisses** as well. Must be something to do with all that Middle Eastern sun, that's what *I* think.

And so it was that Jacob was taken in by his uncle Laban (*literally* – and in more ways than one!).

JACOB SERVES LABAN

WHAT'S IT ALL ABOUT?

This Bible story is about how Jacob got tricked into marrying the wrong woman but then ended up with two wives

WHO ARE THE MAIN CHARACTERS?

Jacob, Laban, Leah and Rachel all compete for star status

WHERE'S IT FOUND IN THE BIBLE?

Genesis 29:15-28

HERE'S THE BIBLE PASSAGE...

Laban said to Jacob, 'You shouldn't work for me for nothing just because you are my relative. How much pay do you want?' Laban had two daughters; the elder was named Leah, and the younger Rachel. Leah had lovely eyes, but Rachel was shapely and beautiful.

Jacob was in love with Rachel, so he said, 'I will work seven years for you, if you will let me marry Rachel.'

Laban answered, 'I would rather give her to you than to anyone else; stay here with me.' Jacob worked seven years so that he could have Rachel, and the time seemed like only a few days to him, because he loved her.

Then Jacob said to Laban, 'The time is up; let me marry your daughter.' So Laban gave a wedding feast and invited everyone. But that night, instead of Rachel, he took Leah to Jacob, and Jacob had intercourse with her. (Laban gave his slave woman Zilpah to his daughter Leah as her maid.) Not until the next morning did Jacob discover that it was Leah. He went to Laban and said, 'Why did you do this to me? I worked to get Rachel. Why have you tricked me?'

Laban answered, 'It is not the custom here to give the younger daughter in marriage before the elder. Wait until the week's marriage celebrations are over, and I will give you Rachel, if you will work for me another seven years.'

Jacob agreed, and when the week of marriage celebrations was over, Laban gave him his daughter Rachel as his wife.

TROUBLE AND STRIFE!

What we've got in *this* story is tale of **trickery** and **deception**. But the person doing the deceiving isn't **Jacob** (who's got a bit of a reputation for that sort of thing) but his **Uncle Laban** who Jacob's staying with in far-flung **Haran**. Well, they *do* say that things run in families, don't they? Jacob was earning his keep by helping out looking after Laban's flocks, but Jacob's generous uncle figured that his nephew should also get *paid* something for all his hard work.

Laban asked Jacob to **name his price**.

But you'll never guess what Jacob *asked* for? He plumped for the hand of **Rachel** (Laban's rather attractive daughter) in marriage. (Well, when I say *hand*, what I *actually* mean is *all* of her – just a hand would be no use to *anybody*, now would it?)

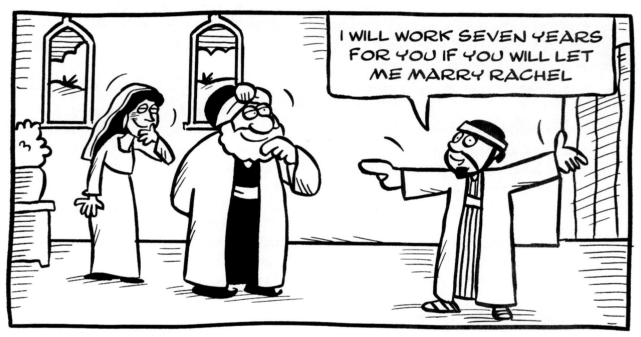

I WILL WORK SEVEN YEARS FOR YOU IF YOU WILL LET ME MARRY RACHEL

Laban was up for it and he agreed to Jacob's pay demand.

The Bible says that the **seven years** only seemed like a **few days** to our Jacob because he was **so much in love**.

Aah! Isn't that *sweet*?

Uncle Laban was as good as his word (or so it *seemed*) and set the wheels in motion for a **whopper of a wedding** for the lovebirds.

I can *only* put it down to the fact that it was dark or that Jacob's bride was wearing a veil 'cos he didn't twig that crafty Laban had **switched the brides**. Jacob ended up getting hitched to Rachel's sister **Leah** (who to be perfectly honest wasn't exactly an oil painting when it came to looks).

Laban's rather *poor* excuse was that it wasn't the custom to marry off the *younger* daughter before the *older* one had got married.

Why he couldn't have told Jacob that **seven years ago**, I *don't* know.

Jacob was not a happy man but Uncle Laban had one *more* cunning ruse up his sleeve.

'Work for me for *another* seven years and you can have **Rachel** as well.'

Jacob agreed to the deal but he didn't have to wait *another* seven long years to marry his beloved Rachel.

He got hitched to her at the end of the marriage celebrations for Leah's wedding.

Don't you just *love* **happy endings**!

JACOB'S BARGAIN WITH LABAN

WHAT'S IT ALL ABOUT?

This Bible story is about Laban's offer to pay Jacob for his hard work and then his attempt to renege on the deal

WHO ARE THE MAIN CHARACTERS?

Jacob and Laban.
Also a many and varied company of sheep and goats

WHERE'S IT FOUND IN THE BIBLE?

Genesis 30:25-43

HERE'S THE BIBLE PASSAGE...

After the birth of Joseph, Jacob said to Laban, 'Let me go, so that I can return home. Give me my wives and children that I have earned by working for you, and I will leave. You know how well I have served you.'

Laban said to him, 'Let me say this: I have learnt by divination that the Lord has blessed me because of you. Name your wages, and I will pay them.'

Jacob answered, 'You know how I have worked for you and how your flocks have prospered under my care. The little you had before I came has grown enormously, and the Lord has blessed you wherever I went. Now it is time for me to look out for my own interests.'

'What shall I pay you?' Laban asked.

Jacob answered, 'I don't want any wages. I will continue to take care of your flocks if you agree to this suggestion: Let me go through all your flocks today and take every black lamb and every spotted or speckled young goat. That is all the wages I want. In the future you can easily find out if I have been honest. When you come to check up on my wages, if I have any goat that isn't speckled or spotted or any sheep that isn't black, you will know that it has been stolen.'

Laban answered, 'Agreed. We will do as you suggest.' But that day Laban removed the male goats that had stripes or spots and all the females that were speckled and spotted or which had white on them; he also removed all the black sheep. He put his sons in charge of them, and then went away from Jacob with this flock as far as he could travel in three days. Jacob took care of the rest of Laban's flocks.

Jacob got green branches of poplar, almond, and plane trees and stripped off some of the bark so that the branches had white stripes on them. He placed these branches in front of the flocks at their drinking troughs. He put them there, because the animals mated when they came to drink. So when the goats bred in front of the branches, they produced young that were streaked, speckled, and spotted.

Jacob kept the sheep separate from the goats and made them face in the direction of the streaked and black animals of Laban's flock. In this way he built up his own flock and kept it apart from Laban's.

When the healthy animals were mating, Jacob put the branches in front of them at the drinking troughs, so that they would breed among the branches. But he did not put the branches in front of the weak animals. Soon Laban had all the weak animals, and Jacob all the healthy ones. In this way Jacob became very wealthy.

He had many flocks, slaves, camels, and donkeys.

DOUBLE-CROSSER!

It had been *yonks* since **Jacob** had been back home to the land of **Canaan** where he came from. He'd settled down with his **Uncle Laban** (not forgetting his two wives, **Leah** and **Rachel**). *Now* he had kids as well and he was getting **itchy feet** to return to the land of his birth.

Laban knew full well that God had been looking after Jacob because things had gone really well for him.

Jacob's uncle told his homesick nephew to name his wages for all the hard work he'd put in on the family farm over the years.

Jacob settled for every **black lamb** and every **speckled** and **spotted goat** from Laban's flocks.

That way Laban would soon know if Jacob (who was inclined to be a bit of a cheat when he wanted to) had diddled his uncle.

But it wasn't *Jacob* who was about to do the diddling but none other than his scheming *uncle*.

That very day he went through his entire flock and took out every goat or sheep that was meant for poor, unsuspecting Jacob.

Then Laban raced off with his sons and got the animals as far as possible from Jacob before he discovered that he'd been **duped** . . .

But unfortunately for Laban it was *Jacob* who had the last laugh. When it came to trickery he wasn't going to be outdone by his **cheating uncle**.

Jacob carefully arranged a collection of **poplar**, **almond** and **plane tree branches** near to where Laban's flocks mated. When the goats bred in front of the branches they gave birth to speckled, streaked and spotted babies.

Don't ask me *how*.

Let's just say that most probably **God** had more than a thing to do with it.

Either way, Jacob got the flock of animals that was coming to him.

In time, Jacob ended up with a **healthy flock** (*and* a healthy bank balance) and his Uncle Laban ended up with a flock of **weak** and **puny animals**.

It looks like Laban had met his match in his nephew Jacob.

JACOB FLEES FROM LABAN

WHAT'S IT ALL ABOUT?

This Bible story is about how Jacob gets to the end of his tether and decides to escape from the clutches of his Uncle Laban

WHO ARE THE MAIN CHARACTERS?

Jacob and his wives, Rachel and Leah. Plus Laban and his angry sons

WHERE'S IT FOUND IN THE BIBLE?

Genesis 31:1-21

HERE'S THE BIBLE PASSAGE...

Jacob heard that Laban's sons were saying, 'Jacob has taken everything that belonged to our father. All his wealth has come from what our father owned.' He also saw that Laban was no longer as friendly as he had been earlier. Then the Lord said to him, 'Go back to the land of your fathers and to your relatives. I will be with you.'

So Jacob sent word to Rachel and Leah to meet him in the field where his flocks were. He said to them, 'I have noticed that your father is not as friendly towards me as he used to be; but my father's God has been with me. You both know that I have worked for your father with all my strength. Yet he has cheated me and changed my wages ten times. But God did not let him harm me. Whenever Laban said, "The speckled goats shall be your wages," all the flocks produced speckled young. When he said, "The striped goats shall be your wages," all the flocks produced striped young. God has taken flocks away from your father and given them to me.

'During the breeding season I had a dream, and I saw that the male goats that were mating were striped, spotted, and speckled. The angel of God spoke to me in the dream and said,

"Jacob!" "Yes," I answered. "Look," he continued, "all the male goats that are mating are striped, spotted, and speckled. I am making this happen because I have seen all that Laban is doing to you. I am the God who appeared to you at Bethel, where you dedicated a stone as a memorial by pouring olive oil on it and where you made a vow to me. Now get ready to go back to the land where you were born." '

Rachel and Leah answered Jacob, 'There is nothing left for us to inherit from our father. He treats us like foreigners. He sold us, and now he has spent all the money he was paid for us. All this wealth which God has taken from our father belongs to us and to our children. Do whatever God has told you.'

So Jacob got ready to go back to his father in the land of Canaan. He put his children and his wives on the camels, and drove all his flocks ahead of him, with everything that he had acquired in Mesopotamia. Laban had gone to shear his sheep, and during his absence Rachel stole the household gods that belonged to her father. Jacob deceived Laban by not letting him know that he was leaving. He took everything he owned and left in a hurry. He crossed the River Euphrates and started for the hill country of Gilead.

QUICK EXIT!

Things weren't looking good for **Jacob**. His uncle (who was also his father-in-law) wasn't too chuffed that his nephew seemed to be getting **richer** by the minute while *his* wealth was rapidly going in the *other* direction.

His flocks weren't *half* as healthy (or numerous) as they used to be in the good old days, but Jacob's were **positively thriving**.

And that didn't please Laban's sons **one little bit**.

They were watching the family business go down the pan before their *very* eyes while their relative (Jacob) seemed to be doing well at the expense of their **dear old dad**.

Tensions were running high and Jacob knew it.

Something had to be done before things turned ugly.

Jacob sent word to his two wives (**Rachel** and **Leah**) that it was time to make a **quick exit** and head back to the land of **Canaan** where he'd come from – before things turned **nasty**.

Jacob arranged to meet up with Rachel and Leah in the field where he kept his flocks . . .

Jacob let his wives in on a little secret. It had been an **angel from God** who'd told him *how* to make his flocks increase. He'd done that because way, way back, many years ago, Jacob had made a promise to worship God.

Rachel and Leah were **100 per cent** behind their hubbie, Jacob, in wanting to leave.

Their dad had been giving *them* a bit of a hard time as well and the way things were going it looked like they were going to end up without a single penny of Laban's wealth.

With Laban out shearing his sheep, Jacob packed his bags, loaded up his camels with his wives and kids and made his **getaway**.

LABAN PURSUES JACOB

WHAT'S IT ALL ABOUT?

This Bible story is about Laban's pursuit of his fleeing nephew (along with his two daughters and his grandchildren)

WHO ARE THE MAIN CHARACTERS?

Jacob and Laban are the key protagonists. Rachel plays a comedic role whilst God also makes a surprise appearance.

WHERE'S IT FOUND IN THE BIBLE?

Genesis 31:22-49

HERE'S THE BIBLE PASSAGE...

Three days later Laban was told that Jacob had fled. He took his men with him and pursued Jacob for seven days until he caught up with him in the hill country of Gilead.

In a dream that night God came to Laban and said to him, 'Be careful not to threaten Jacob in any way.' Jacob had set up his camp on a mountain, and Laban set up his camp with his relatives in the hill country of Gilead.

Laban said to Jacob, 'Why did you deceive me and carry off my daughters like women captured in war? Why did you deceive me and slip away without telling me? If you had told me, I would have sent you on your way with rejoicing and singing to the music of tambourines and harps. You did not even let me kiss my grandchildren and my daughters goodbye. That was a foolish thing to do! I have the power to do you harm, but last night the God of your father warned me not to threaten you in any way. I know that you left because you were so anxious to get back home, but why did you steal my household gods?'

Jacob answered, 'I was afraid, because I thought that you might take your daughters away from me. But if you find that anyone here has your gods, he will be put to death. Here, with our men as witnesses, look for anything that belongs to you and take what is yours.' Jacob did not know that Rachel had stolen Laban's gods.

Laban went and searched Jacob's tent; then he went into Leah's tent, and the tent of the two slave women, but he did not find his gods. Then he went into Rachel's tent. Rachel had taken the household gods and put them in a camel's saddlebag and was sitting on them. Laban searched through the whole tent, but did not find them. Rachel said to her father, 'Do not be angry with me, sir, but I am not able to stand up in your presence; I am having my monthly period.' Laban searched but did not find his household gods.

Then Jacob lost his temper. 'What crime have I committed?' he asked angrily. 'What law have I broken that gives you the right to hunt me down? Now that you have searched through all my belongings, what household article have you found that belongs to you? Put it out here where your men and mine can see it, and let them decide which one of us is right. I have been with you now for twenty years; your sheep and your goats have not failed to reproduce, and I have not eaten any rams from your flocks.

'Whenever a sheep was killed by wild animals, I always bore the loss myself. I didn't take it to you to show that it was not my fault. You demanded that I make good anything that was stolen during the day or during the night. Many times I suffered from the heat during the day and from the cold at night. I was not able to sleep. It was like that for the whole twenty years I was with you. For fourteen years I worked to win your two daughters – and six years for your flocks. And even then, you changed my wages ten times. If the God of my fathers, the God of Abraham and Isaac, had not been with me, you would have already sent me away empty-handed. But God has seen my trouble and the work I have done, and last night he gave his judgement.' Laban answered Jacob, 'These young women are my daughters; their children belong to me, and these flocks are mine. In fact, everything you see here belongs to me. But since I can do nothing to keep my daughters and their children, I am ready to make an agreement with you. Let us make a pile of stones to remind us of our agreement.' So Jacob took a stone and set it up as a memorial. He told his men to gather some rocks and pile them up. Then they ate a meal beside the pile of rocks. Laban named it Jegar Sahadutha, while Jacob named it Galeed. Laban said to Jacob, 'This pile of rocks will be a reminder for both of us.' That is why that place was named Galeed. Laban also said, 'May the Lord keep an eye on us while we are separated from each other.'

GOTCHA!

Laban was a bit of a **crook** at heart but he didn't particularly like it when somebody got the better of *him*. And that's *exactly* what his nephew **Jacob** had done. Along with his wives (Laban's *daughters*) his kids and his flocks, Jacob had run *away* from Laban, who had been his employer for more years than he cared to remember. Jacob's uncle Laban had tried to trick Jacob out of his wages (**sheep and goats**) for all his years of hard work but Jacob had hatched his *own* cunning plan to get what was **rightfully his**.

Because Jacob knew that Laban wouldn't be too happy about that, he'd made a quick getaway in the direction of **Canaan** where he was originally from. Are you with me still? Good!

It took Laban **three days** to realise that Jacob had done a runner but he wasted no time in setting off, hot foot, to catch his **runaway nephew**.

After a **seven-day chase** Laban and his men caught up with Jacob. Before he'd had the chance to get his hands on Jacob God had a word with him (in a dream) . . .

BE CAREFUL NOT TO THREATEN JACOB IN ANY WAY

Well *that* couldn't be clearer, now, could it? Isn't it great when you've got **God** on your side.

At a place called **Gilead** Laban and Jacob finally came **face to face**.

Laban accused Jacob of kidnapping his daughters and deceiving him when all along *he'd* been the one doing the deceiving. Then, to top it all, he went so far as to suggest that he'd have given Jacob a big send off. **As if!**

What Jacob *didn't* know was that one of his wives (**Rachel**) had nicked her dad's **household gods**. Laban didn't worship the same God as Jacob. He worshipped *man-made* gods (or statues) which he believed would bring him good luck. When he'd discovered that they'd gone missing at precisely the same time that Jacob and co. had left he put two and two together and figured that his *nephew* must be the **culprit**.

Jacob let Laban hunt through all his tents, one by one, but without any success. That was because Rachel had hidden the household gods in her **camel's saddlebag** and was sitting on them.

Jacob eventually called a halt to Laban's investigations. He'd had *enough* of his uncle meddling with his affairs. It was time to part company. Laban agreed not to pursue Jacob any longer and to seal the deal the pair of them plonked a **pile of stones** down where they stood as a handy reminder.

And so they parted company, Jacob heading for a new life in **Canaan** and Laban back to **Haran** where he'd come from.

JACOB WRESTLES WITH GOD

WHAT'S IT ALL ABOUT?

This Bible story is about when Jacob goes a few rounds with God and how it changes his life for ever

WHO ARE THE MAIN CHARACTERS?

Jacob and an angel from God (or perhaps even God himself) share the stage

WHERE'S IT FOUND IN THE BIBLE?

Genesis 32:22-32

HERE'S THE BIBLE PASSAGE...

That same night Jacob got up, took his two wives, his two concubines, and his eleven children, and crossed the River Jabbok. After he had sent them across, he also sent across all that he owned, but he stayed behind, alone.

Then a man came and wrestled with him until just before daybreak. When the man saw that he was not winning the struggle, he struck Jacob on the hip, and it was thrown out of joint. The man said, 'Let me go; daylight is coming.'

'I won't, unless you bless me,' Jacob answered.

'What is your name?' the man asked. 'Jacob,' he answered.

The man said, 'Your name will no longer be Jacob. You have struggled with God and with men, and you have won; so your name will be Israel.'

Jacob said, 'Now tell me your name.'

But he answered, 'Why do you want to know my name?' Then he blessed Jacob.

Jacob said, 'I have seen God face to face, and I am still alive'; so he named the place Peniel. The sun rose as Jacob was leaving Peniel, and he was limping because of his hip. Even today the descendants of Israel do not eat the muscle which is on the hip joint, because it was on this muscle that Jacob was struck.

THE BIG FIGHT!

This Bible story is all about a guy called **Jacob**. He's hardly had what you could call a quiet life and things *weren't* about to change. He'd spent most of his life **on the run** or **falling out** with people but there was more to come. Jacob was headed back to the land of **Canaan** where he'd tricked his elder brother **Esau** out of his inheritance. (Well, to be fair to Jacob, Esau had sort of *sold* it to Jacob for a **plate of stew** but that's *another* story.)

A return trip to Canaan meant meeting up with Esau again and that's something Jacob *wasn't* looking forward to in the slightest.

Jacob might have had a few rough edges but **God** had actually **hand-picked** him to head up a special nation of people who worshipped God.

Jacob probably figured that he needed a bit of time alone with God because the Bible says that Jacob sent his whole family and flocks on ahead of him (across the river Jabbok) while he spent the night with God. What Jacob *hadn't* bargained on was a **wrestling match** with God.

Perhaps it was an angel from God – who knows? *Either* way, Jacob had a fight on his hands.

When Jacob seemed to be getting the *better* of his opponent, he put Jacob's hip out of joint. **Ouch!**

Jacob *got* the blessing he was asking for and the person he was fighting announced that from now on he wouldn't be called Jacob – he'd be called **Israel** (which means '**he struggles with God**'. How appropriate!) Then God left him.

As the sun came up, it dawned on Jacob that he'd seen God **face to face** and was *still* alive.

He was one *lucky* Jacob.

And he wasn't the scheming Jacob any more – the Jacob who'd cheated on his brother and tricked his uncle to get his own way.

Jacob (or **Israel** as he was now called) was a man who now **relied on God 100 per cent**. I suppose *that's* why he wouldn't let God go all through the night. From now on he'd cling on to God *whatever* happened.

As for that **painful hip**. OK, so it had left him with a **limp** but it was *also* a permanent reminder of his mega meeting with God.

JACOB MEETS ESAU

WHAT'S IT ALL ABOUT?

This Bible story is about the extremely tense reunion between Jacob and his twin brother Esau

WHO ARE THE MAIN CHARACTERS?

Jacob and Esau. But there's an epic cast of Esau's 400 men and Jacob's huge entourage of family and flocks

WHERE'S IT FOUND IN THE BIBLE?

Genesis 33:1-17

HERE'S THE BIBLE PASSAGE...

Jacob saw Esau coming with his 400 men, so he divided the children among Leah, Rachel and the two concubines. He put the concubines and their children first, then Leah and her children, and finally Rachel and Joseph at the rear. Jacob went ahead of them and bowed down to the ground seven times as he approached his brother. But Esau ran to meet him, threw his arms round him, and kissed him. They were both crying. When Esau looked round and saw the women and the children, he asked, 'Who are these people with you?'

'These, sir, are the children whom God has been good enough to give me,' Jacob answered. Then the concubines came up with their children and bowed down; then Leah and her children came, and last of all Joseph and Rachel came and bowed down.

Esau asked, 'What about that other group I met? What did that mean?'

Jacob answered, 'It was to gain your favour.'

But Esau said, 'I have enough, my brother; keep what you have.'

Jacob said, 'No, please, if I have gained your favour, accept my gift. To see your face is for me like seeing the face of God, now that you have been so friendly to me. Please accept this gift which I have brought for you; God has been kind to me and given me everything I need.' Jacob kept on urging him until he accepted.

Esau said, 'Let's prepare to leave. I will go ahead of you.'

Jacob answered, 'You know that the children are weak, and I must think of the sheep and cattle with their young. If they are driven hard for even one day, the whole herd will die. Please go on ahead of me, and I will follow slowly, going as fast as I can with the livestock and the children until I catch up with you in Edom.'

Esau said, 'Then let me leave some of my men with you.'

But Jacob answered, 'There is no need for that for I only want to gain your favour.' So that day Esau started on his way back to Edom. But Jacob went to Sukkoth, where he built a house for himself and shelters for his livestock.

O BROTHER!

Have you ever seen one of those **TV shows** where long-lost relatives are reunited? Well that's *exactly* what's about to occur in *this* Bible bit but as far as **Jacob** (the star of the story) is concerned, he's not expecting a good reception from his twin brother **Esau**.

They'd fallen out a *long* time ago . . . and guess who was the cause. Yep! It was *Jacob*.

Esau had always been the rough-tough one and Jacob could only imagine that Esau was now about to settle old scores and get his *own* back on his **cheating brother Jacob**.

Which is why Jacob wasn't going to take any chances.

He's already sent an advance party ahead to soften Esau up but he *still* wasn't going to risk a *thing*.

Jacob split his wives and kids into groups for their protection and then ran out to meet Esau (**and his 400 men**) . . .

While Jacob was grovelling on the ground, Esau raced up to his long-lost twin and flung his arms around him. No, he *wasn't* trying to throttle him. In fact Esau even went as far as to *kiss* Jacob. (**Yuk!**)

Esau wasn't angry at all.

He was **over the moon** at seeing his little brother again. Jacob must have sighed a big sigh of relief.

As far as *Esau* was concerned he wanted to **let bygones be bygones**. All *he* was interested in was being introduced to Jacob's wives and kids.

(Just think of those **birthday pressies** he'd now have to buy.)

After a bit of gentle persuasion, Esau accepted Jacob's gift of a nice selection of animals.

(Not gift-wrapped though – *that* would take *forever.*)

Esau was *itching* to take Jacob back home but Jacob, his family and flocks were worn out from their long journey. They needed time to recuperate. So *instead*, Jacob and Esau agreed to part company and then to meet up again in a place called **Edom**.

Phew! What a day *that* was. I'll bet Jacob slept a lot better *that* night.

JACOB GOES TO BETHEL

WHAT'S IT ALL ABOUT?

This Bible story is about Jacob's (and his family's) arrival in Canaan and the side-effects of them getting right with God

WHO ARE THE MAIN CHARACTERS?

Jacob and God (who appears to him). His family, who get a minor mention, and last, but not least – a rock

WHERE'S IT FOUND IN THE BIBLE?

Genesis 35:1-15

HERE'S THE BIBLE PASSAGE...

God said to Jacob, 'Go to Bethel at once, and live there. Build an altar there to me, the God who appeared to you when you were running away from your brother Esau.'

So Jacob said to his family and to all who were with him, 'Get rid of the foreign gods that you have; purify yourselves and put on clean clothes. We are going to leave here and go to Bethel, where I will build an altar to the God who helped me in the time of my trouble and who has been with me everywhere I have gone.' So they gave Jacob all the foreign gods that they had and also the earrings that they were wearing. He buried them beneath the oak tree near Shechem.

When Jacob and his sons started to leave, great fear fell on the people of the nearby towns, and they did not pursue them. Jacob came with all his people to Luz, which is now known as Bethel, in the land of Canaan. He built an altar there and named the place after the God of Bethel, because God had revealed himself to him there when he was running away from his brother. Rebecca's nurse Deborah died and was buried beneath the oak south of Bethel. So it was named 'Oak of Weeping'.

When Jacob returned from Mesopotamia, God appeared to him again and blessed him. God said to him, 'Your name is Jacob, but from now on it will be Israel.' So God named him Israel. And God said to him, 'I am Almighty God. Have many children. Nations will be descended from you, and you will be the ancestor of kings. I will give you the land which I gave to Abraham and to Isaac, and I will also give it to your descendants after you.' Then God left him. There, where God had spoken to him, Jacob set up a memorial stone and consecrated it by pouring wine and olive oil on it. He named the place Bethel.

CLEAN-UP TIME!

It's funny how *some* people seem to spend half their life roaming all over the world but then **end up** exactly where they **started**. **Jacob** was a bit like that. (OK, so he'd roamed as far as **Mesopotamia**, but that was a long way in *those* days.)

Now he was back in the land of **Canaan** where he'd come from.

Jacob didn't need to hunt round estate agents looking for a place to live. He went one *better*.

God told *him* where to settle. And **Bethel** was the name of the place he was to live in but what's even *more* amazing is that Jacob was the one who'd given Bethel it's name in the first place – many years ago.

That's because Jacob had a rather awesome **meeting with God** there, and now here he was, right back where he'd *started*.

God had told Jacob to build an **altar** to him there but *first* there were a few things Jacob needed to put right . . .

> GET RID OF THE FOREIGN GODS THAT YOU HAVE. PURIFY YOURSELVES WITH CLEAN CLOTHES. WE ARE GOING TO BETHEL WHERE I WILL BUILD AN ALTAR TO GOD WHO HAS BEEN WITH ME EVERYWHERE I HAVE GONE!

Jacob's wives had brought with them a *load* of stuff to do with the gods they worshipped in Mesopotamia but Jacob's God was having *none* of it.

If God was going to use Jacob to head up a special nation of people who worshipped him (which is what the plan was) then Jacob's *family* had to be **all out for God** as well. It's *amazing* what happens when you obey God.

As soon as Jacob's family had cleaned up their lives the Bible tells us that all the people who lived nearby were **terrified**.

It was as if they could **feel God's presence** around Jacob and his family – and they were completely **overwhelmed** by it.

Jacob built his altar to God and then God turned up (like he'd done before) and reminded Jacob of all his **promises** to him; for example, that he would have many nations descended from him and that he would give the land of Canaan to Jacob *and* his descendants.

A long time ago, Jacob had set up a **stone** as a reminder that Bethel was where he'd met with God.

Well, that's just what our Jacob did *again*. (Funny how history repeats itself.) And just like he'd done before, Jacob poured **olive oil** over it to tell God how special he thought he was.

ALSO AVAILABLE

from John Hunt Publishing Ltd
46a West Street, New Alresford, Hampshire, SO24 9AU
www.johnhunt-publishing.com